4016

PSYCHOLOGY OF MISSIONARY ADJUSTMENT

Marge Jones with E. Grant Jones

Stanley M. Horton, Th. D.
General Editor

LOGION PRESS

Springfield, Missouri
02-0321

2nd Printing 2000

Logion Press books are published by Gospel Publishing House.

Library of Congress Cataloging-in-Publication Data

Jones, Marge, 1929–
Psychology of missionary adjustment / Marge Jones with E. Grant Jones; Stanley M. Horton, general editor
　　p.　cm.
Includes bibliographical references and index.
ISBN 0-88243-321-0
1. Missionaries—Psychology. 2. Missions—Theory. 3. Psychology, Religious. I. Jones, E. Grant, 1956– . II. Horton, Stanley M. III. Title.
BV2094.6.J66　　1994
266'.0019—dc20　　　　　　　　　　　　　　　94–36181

Printed in the United States of America

Contents

Foreword

For some people, the words "psychology" and "missionary adjustment" do not belong in the same sentence, let alone in the title of a book. According to their view, psychology has nothing to do with being a successful missionary. Why would a missionary, of all people, need psychology? Besides, if missionaries need to adjust, let them read their Bibles and pray, and God will meet their needs.

That rather simplistic view of life in general, and especially of missionary work, rests on the assumption that Christians have nothing to gain—and much to lose—from using psychology. Although the church shunned psychology in its beginnings (for good reason in some cases), gradually Christians have come to accept that the God-given psychological insights into people and their problems, used according to biblical values and standards, can bring help and healing to many people. That was a big hurdle for many Christians, but perhaps an even bigger one is to accept the reality that missionaries also need help. Every missionary breakdown is a loss for the individual, the family, the church, and the work of Christ around the world. But rarely do we acknowledge that the pressures of missionary life and ministry actually increase the potential for breakdowns. That's because American Christians have little understanding of how hard it is to be a missionary, cut off from many of the resources

6

we take for granted and exposed as never before to all the powers of darkness. They also fail to understand that missionaries take their emotional problems with them. Many times these problems have been buried, but in the cauldron of living in a different culture with many different pressures, these problems flare into the open.

People who send out and pray for missionaries do have a high view of them. Therefore, they assume that missionaries will be totally dedicated to evangelism, teaching, medical work, and so on, and will not be bothered by the kinds of problems that beset ordinary Christians. The truth is, dedication does not prevent emotional disasters from happening on the field. People with the greatest zeal and the highest sense of being called by God to serve Him overseas do stumble and fall.

Once we get past the word "psychology" we come to grips with another basic fact of missionary life—adjustment. Moving from Atlanta to Seattle requires adjustment. On a much more intense level, moving from the United States to another country and culture requires adjustment. That's because world missions is not an export business. It's not like shipping computers from here to Brazil. Missionaries and their lives and ministries cannot be "Fed Exed" from here to there. Missionaries from one country do not fit in another, no matter how well prepared, how thoroughly trained and educated, and how highly motivated. They don't fit because they don't speak the same language, eat the same food, or follow the same customs and habits of etiquette.

Too many missionaries have stumbled because they could not handle the difficulties of adjustment. Too many have continued to live overseas without becoming part of the local culture. They maintain an American cocoon to keep themselves from as much of the local culture as they can. They fail as missionaries, even though they do not come home. They are not willing to pay the price of adjustment. They do not love but rather criticize things dear to local people.

If that doesn't make the task difficult enough, missionaries then have to work out their ministry assignments, how they fit into the local church, how they relate to other missionaries, and how they grow together in their own families. Single missionaries have their unique set of adjustments. Each one of these matters requires growth and development, most of it painful because people and their feelings are easily bruised. Missionaries learn much about themselves when they are thrown into cross-cultural adjustment.

For these reasons, the kind of book written by Marge Jones is absolutely essential. She has successfully blended her experiences and insights gained from many years of service on the field with her sound knowledge of how people can live together and be successful on the mission field. Yes, hers is a wonderfully practical book of applied psychology from both a Christian and a missionary viewpoint.

Churches and schools at home need to prepare future missionaries along the lines of her work. Missionaries already on the field will be greatly helped by Marge's wise counsel. She addresses the critical issues with a desire to bring healing, to save missionary careers, and to guide those on the way to service overseas. The world missions enterprise will be strengthened by her love and wisdom.

JIM REAPSOME
Editor
Evangelical Missions Quarterly

Preface

A great missionary quit last week.

Resigned, just like that. After two terms on the field. After learning two languages. After adjusting to the culture. After learning to live with 120-degree heat, flies, mosquitoes, dirt, bugs, and plenty of sand. After living through several government coups. After acquiring cross-cultural communication skills.

He loved the people with whom he was working. He loved them vicariously before he ever met them and continued to love them after seeing them as they were, not through rose-colored glasses but through a magnifying glass. He loved eating their food, living in their homes, worshiping in their churches, singing their songs.

He bought his food in the local noisy, crowded market where flies covered the meat and the smell of dried fish covered the air. He knew which hole-in-the-wall store would have washers for leaky faucets, wire for blown fuses, or spark plugs for the car. He had learned to belong.

What about the years of preparation—Bible school, pastoring a struggling church, itineration with the desperate need to raise the budget in the allotted time, and language study? The long months of frustration trying to remember how to conjugate irregular verbs or pronounce sounds that never seemed to come out right? And the cost? A missions executive told me that it costs their mission over two hundred thousand dollars to get a couple to the field the first time!

But dollars are replaceable—human lives aren't.

No, you will never find his name in history of missions books. The people whose lives he impacted don't write books. He never conducted a large tent crusade. He wasn't shot during the military coups. He never managed to make the spotlight. He just did the job he was given to do. Or thought he was to do.

But something went wrong, tragically wrong. Does the missions department know what happened? I don't know. Surveys indicate that missionaries don't always give the deep-down, inside reason for quitting.

A great missionary quit last week. Someone else will probably go to take his place. If this book helps that someone to persevere through the second, third, fourth, and even fifth term, should Jesus tarry, then every long hour spent in its preparation and writing has been well spent.

Introduction

"Those who are interested in psychology and missions have yet to develop and pursue a concerted and coordinated direction of research," reported William F. Hunter and Marvin K. Mayers in "Psychology and Missions: Reflections on Status and Need."[1] Although psychological and psychiatric services have been used for a number of years in the process of selecting missionaries for service outside the United States, a constant and continuing study of the effects of overseas living on all aspects of the missionary's adjustment has been lacking. Specific areas have been treated in depth, such as culture shock,[2] language study,[3] children's education,[4] interfamily and interpersonnel relationships and reentry.[5] In this book an attempt is made to look at the total psychological problem of missionary adjustment, from the moment of feeling a "call" to the "foreign field" (a country outside the borders of the United States) to the ultimate time of retirement.

All mission boards, whether evangelical or traditional, Protestant or Catholic, would agree with John Miner[6] that people "are the essential ingredient in all organizations—be they business, educational, governmental, or religious—and the ways people are recruited and utilized by the leadership largely determine whether the organization will survive and achieve its objectives." The complexities of living in a culture and working with people whose mores are not only different but also often opposite those of the individual require a diverse and in-depth training program.

A college student planning a career in personnel management would study courses in industrial sociology, labor economics, industrial engineering, labor law, industrial medicine, and industrial psychology, all courses dealing with interpersonal and employee-management relations. Most missions majors receive in-depth training in biblical studies and theology, some cross-cultural communication courses, and, in some cases, anthropology. Yet the problems that arise on the mission field seldom have to do with theology or communicating the biblical message. Missionaries are seldom asked to leave the field by the national church because of a lack of theological communication. Almost invariably missionaries quit the field or are requested to leave because of their lack of internal, or psychological, adjustment to a situation they are unwilling or unable to accept or for which no compromise can be found.

The following definitions are given for the terms used in this book to establish a frame of reference and to avoid misunderstanding their meanings.

PSYCHOLOGY

The *Oxford English Dictionary* defines psychology as "the science of the nature, functions, and phenomena of the human soul or mind." The term comes from two Greek words, *psuchē* ("soul") and *logos* ("word" or "discourse"), so the original meaning was a discourse about the soul and, later, the mind. As an applied science, then, psychology could be defined as the scientific study of behavior and mental processes.[7]

We agree with E. Rae Harcum[8] when he claims that psychologists investigate why human beings act the way they do and attempt to use this knowledge to improve their behavior (that is, if by "behavior" he means the individual's adjustment to a situation he or she cannot manipulate as well as the situation he can). But in a much broader sense, as one of the behavioral sciences, psychology "probe[s] the various individual and corporate parameters of human behavior."[9]

In this book the meaning of psychology will be limited to the understanding of human nature in the unique situations requiring specific modes of adjustment to a non-North American setting.

MISSIONARY

The term "missionary" refers to any person who works full-time for a religious organization outside the borders of the home country and whose primary purpose is to communicate the gospel as revealed in the Bible. Missionaries may be in professions such as medicine, education, construction, agriculture, translation, and transport, but their goal through their service is to convert people to Christianity—just like their clergy counterparts—as church-planters, pastors, and evangelists. Since national churches (organizations having national leadership and administration recognized by local governments) have already been established in many mission fields, it is possible that a majority of missionary personnel are now involved in what is termed "support ministries" rather than preaching ministries. Local people have been trained and are functioning as pastors, evangelists, church-planters, and administrators.

A growing number of Christian volunteers spend short terms (two weeks to two years) in specialized ministries overseas and are typically referred to as "missionaries." Although their duties may be the same as those of career missionaries, their adjustment process is not. They know that whatever local situation exists, their time in it is limited; they can escape rather than adjust. A career missionary doesn't have this option. Even if he or she withdraws or is withdrawn from one situation, there will likely be more of the same type of problem in the new location.

MISSION FIELD

"Mission field" refers to any country outside the territorial borders of the home country. In most cases it would be considered a developing country, referred to as being in the "third world" by the popular press. At the same time, a developed country, even though it may have a standard of living that equals or exceeds that of the United States, also represents a process of adjustment to a different code of ethics and social mores.

ADJUSTMENT

What constitutes adjustment? In his book on personal adjustment, Harold Bernard[10] defines adjustment as "a process rather than an achievement. It does, indeed, include for some people giving up themselves and doing what society, their peers, or parents hope for and expect. . . . Adjustment must include mutual accommodation."

Perhaps "mutual accommodation" best describes the psychological adjustment process of today's career missionary. Rarely do missionary personnel live under exactly the same conditions as the majority of those they are working among in developing countries. (Refer to chapter 4, "Bonding," for more discussion of this topic.) In any case, wearing the national dress, eating the national dishes, and living in the same conditions as most of the nationals does not make a national out of a missionary. Value systems and thought processes are not the same. An understanding and acceptance of the reasoning processes and methodology of the people the missionary is working among is necessary for actual adjustment to take place. In other words, being able to think like the national is a better indication of adjustment than merely looking like the national.

TRADITIONAL PROTESTANT ORGANIZATIONS

Traditional Protestant organizations are those denominations affiliated with the World Council of Churches. They are often referred to as "conciliar" Protestant churches, many having been in existence since the Reformation. Generally they practice a fixed liturgy and in recent years have been more involved in the social aspect of missions than in evangelization. Examples are the Presbyterian, Methodist, and Lutheran organizations.[11]

EVANGELICAL ORGANIZATIONS

Evangelical church organizations are those belonging to the National Association of Evangelicals.[12] Although involved in social work on the mission field, their main purpose is the conversion of non-Christians to Christianity. They generally believe in the inerrancy of the Bible, water baptism by immersion, the expiatory work of Christ's death on the cross, a literal heaven and hell, and the eternal damnation of all who do not accept salvation through faith in Jesus Christ.

Several Pentecostal church organizations belong in this category. They believe that the manifestations of the Holy Spirit mentioned in the New Testament are for all Christians today. They consider the baptism, or infilling, of the Holy Spirit an experience separate from salvation and actively seek the gifts of the Spirit mentioned by the apostle Paul in his epistles.

Another term used for those who hold these Pentecostal beliefs is "charismatics." They generally belong to independent churches (those not affiliated with any organized denomination) or form groups in organized denominations. They seldom have an organized missions endeavor but may send out individual missionaries totally supported by one or two churches. Even so, these missionaries often work under the supervision of an organized missions board.

NONDENOMINATIONAL ORGANIZATIONS

A number of mission organizations exist on the mission field that are not affiliated with any denomination. They accept candidates from all churches who are willing to work under their authority, rules, and doctrinal statement. They were organized for the specific purpose of evangelization and church planting on the mission field. Their funding comes mainly from churches in the United States, Canada, and Great Britain with no denominational affiliation.

PARACHURCH ORGANIZATIONS

There are also several nondenominational organizations that, although they do evangelize, exist as support systems. Known as parachurch groups, they work mainly in air transportation in remote areas, translation, and socioeconomic endeavors, which they make available to all missions.

---

[1]William F. Hunter and Marvin K. Mayers, "Psychology and Missions: Reflections on Status and Need," *Journal of Psychology and Theology* 15 (Winter 1987), 269–73.

[2]Myron Loss, *Culture Shock: Dealing with Stress in Cross-Cultural Living* (Winona Lake, Ind.: Light and Life Press, 1983).

[3]Donald N. Larson, *Guidelines for Barefoot Language Learning* (St. Paul: CMS Publishing, 1984).

[4]Pam Echerd and Alice Arathoon, eds. *Planning for MK Nurture.* Vol. 2 (Pasadena, Calif.: William Carey Library, 1989). C. John Buffam, *The Life and Times of an MK* (Pasadena, Calif.: William Carey Library, 1985).

[5]Marjory F. Foyle, *Overcoming Missionary Stress.* (Wheaton, Ill.: Evangelical Missions Information Service, 1987). Kelly S. O'Donnell and Michele Lewis O'Donnell, eds. *Helping Missionaries Grow: Readings in Mental Health and Missions* (Pasadena, Calif.: William Carey Library, 1988).

[6]John B. Miner, *Personnel Psychology* (London: Collier-Macmillan, 1969), 1.

[7]Diane E. Papalia and Sally W. Olds, *Psychology* (New York: McGraw-Hill, 1988), 5.

[8]E. Rae Harcum, *Psychology for Daily Living* (Chicago: Nelson-Hall, 1979), 2.

[9]Hunter and Mayers, "Psychology and Missions," 269–73.

[10]Harold W. Bernard and Wesley C. Huckins, *Dynamics of Personal Adjustment,* 2d ed. (Boston: Holbrook Press, Inc., 1975), preface.

[11]Information can be obtained from the World Council of Churches, 150 route de Ferney, 1211 Geneva 2, Switzerland.

[12]Information can be obtained from the National Association of Evangelicals, P. O. Box 28, Wheaton, IL 60187.

Chapter One

The Pedestal

Almost two thousand years ago the Holy Spirit said to the church in Antioch, Syria, "'Set apart for me Barnabas and Saul for the work to which I have called them'" (Acts 13:2). Thus started the first recorded missionary endeavor of the Christian church. The "call" came from God to individuals who were worshiping and to a body of believers who were willing to do God's bidding.

Missionary work is unique in that the individual has felt a specific urge, or prompting, from God to focus on a specific country or task. In many cases a definite spiritual experience is involved. Monetary, safety, and security factors become secondary to the desire to accomplish what is considered God's purpose.

As the following testimonies show, the individual can feel the prompting of God in a number of ways.

"While I was in a missions prayer group, God told me to go to this country in Africa. I thought this was foolish, because all of Africa was Tarzan country to me. But I couldn't get away from the feeling. . . . I finally arrived on the last flight before the airport was closed [because of political problems]."

"A missionary lady came to our church and told about the work she was doing. From that day, I knew that God wanted me to go to that place and work for Him."

"One night at youth camp as I was praying, I saw a bright light and heard a voice saying, 'I want you to be my missionary.'"

When God told the church in Antioch to "set apart" Saul and Barnabas, He did not indicate that they should be treated in any special way. They were not set on a pedestal to be admired as unique. They were believers, led by the Holy Spirit, to accomplish God's purpose for their lives, which is the will of God for all who are followers of Jesus Christ. Unfortunately, an individual today who feels called to missionary service is often set on a pedestal by other believers because of a willingness to give up living in the home country for the sake of the mission field.

VOCATION

It is hard to assess the psychological impact of a vocation, or special calling, on a person's ego or self-concept. The ego, as defined by Harold Bernard and Wesley Huckins, comprises "those elements of the personality responsible for perceiving, knowing, reasoning, feeling, deciding, and doing." Three aspects are involved in an individual's self-understanding:

1. self-as-subject, or what the person thinks of himself or herself.
2. self-as-object, or what others think of the person.
3. self-as-process or action, such as manipulating, perceiving, and thinking.[1]

Any vocation, or call, involves two separate choices: God's choice of the person and the person's choice to accept what is perceived as God's call. This presupposes the concept of a personal relationship with God, that it is possible to hear, audibly or inaudibly, His voice. Some individuals have expressed this as a humbling experience, that God considered them worthy of a special task. However, the very notion of being "chosen" sets a person apart, in a unique category. Consciously or unconsciously the individual has been set on a pedestal by the family, the church, and the community. Different from the norm, those who respond to the call are willing to sacrifice their own desires for the greater good of humankind.

The influence of family on a person's vocation cannot be ignored. Probably many Irish Catholic families would be proud to have one of their children feel a vocation to the priesthood or a convent as the culmination of conversations around the dinner table. Missionary parents feel rewarded when their children decide to become missionaries. The experiences their children had on the field were not negative but became the basis for their choice of future ministry. Rarely mentioned but often present in the subconscious is the thought, *We did something right—look at our child!*

The influence of the church is also strong. Emotionally charged missionary services, where an appeal is given after a stirring message highlighting the needs of the mission field, bring many to dedicate themselves to overseas ministry. For these people, as well as for many others who become career missionaries, the need constitutes the call. Some organizations publish papers that list specific service needs on the field, such as those of a doctor, contractor, or teacher. Although these people may be considered recruited rather than called, the psychological effect is probably much the same. They are still set apart for a special assignment.

Family, church, and peers probably influence the individual's self-image. Carl Rogers, a noted therapist who has done research on self-concept, feels that one's self-perception results from one's interaction with other people. If considered "special" by close associates, a person may then well feel specially equipped by God for what lies ahead.[2]

Rather than being a hindrance, this self-concept can be of vital importance to one's dedication and perseverance in living out a difficult lifestyle. The conscious decision to forfeit a life of relative ease, of security with family and friends, for unknown conditions in an unknown part of the world, working with unknown people, demands considerable self-confidence, which can certainly be a product of feeling "special."

Another product of the pedestal effect could be the development of control mechanisms, actions used to influence one's environment. If these actions satisfy a need, they tend to become part of an individual's repertoire and are repeated whenever that control is needed. One often acquires this behavior without being aware of its effect.[3]

Individuals who want to become missionaries exert an influence over their families (spouse, children, or parents) to persuade them that their vocation is genuine. They must also influence their home church and pastor for their financial support as well as their denomination for their candidacy. Without exerting these control mechanisms, it would be virtually impossible to accomplish the myriad tasks necessary to arrive on the field. "Perseverance" could be the term used for such actions, probably a necessary part of the psychological repertoire of an effective missionary.

However, these control mechanisms used so effectively for getting to the field can become a detriment to relationships with national pastors and missionary colleagues. (See chapter 9, "Conflicts.") Individuals will have to accept many decisions that are beyond their control and with which they do not agree, while at the same time preserving their self-confidence. Adjustment to missionary life may be very difficult for persons with a fragile ego structure or unyielding control mechanisms, because they will have to live and work under many conditions that will be beyond their control.

Individuals placed on a pedestal because of their call to the mission field need to understand how much this treatment has influenced their thoughts and actions and how detrimental the results can be when they arrive overseas. They also need to realize that there may be a long, and often arduous, process before their vocation can be achieved.

SELECTION

In most denominations, the selection process starts with an individual's application to a mission board, the authorized administrative body governing missionary activity. After the application is received, the individual or couple is invited to meet with the board. The impressions made at this meeting are of vital importance, for the board and the missionary will of necessity have a close relationship. The board sets the policies the missionary will have to follow. The board generally controls the finances and often the field assignment of the missionary. Disciplinary action is usually under the control of the board.

Candidates are generally under a great deal of tension when they meet the board. Although they are sure God has considered them worthy, the board might not. If, during the application process, the candidates could informally meet members of the board one to one, before the formal board meeting, probably much of the stress could be eliminated. The members of the board would also have a more reliable impression to base their decision on.

Besides considering the application forms and personal contact, the board will consider a number of other factors. Some organizations now use psychological tests such as the Taylor-Johnson Temperament Analysis, California Psychological Inventory, the Minnesota Multiphasic Personality Inventory-2, the Fundamental Interpersonal Relations Orientation-Behavior, and the Millan Clinical Multiaxial Inventory II.[4]

The average age of candidates in the 1980s and 1990s seems to be five to ten years older than those thirty to forty years ago. Educational requirements are higher in many cases, both those set by the mission board and by the country the candidates will be going to; many developing countries no longer give resident visas to missionaries doing pastoral, evangelistic, or church-planting work.

Even so, on many (if not most) fields, a national church has been established which is no longer in need of assistance in these areas. Some type of social or educational ministry is usually required by the mission board, necessitating specialized training of the candidate. The missionaries work along with or under the direction of the national church, which is the authority. Governments grant or withhold visas according to the wishes of the national church.

Many mission boards have established age limits for accepting candidates. Pressure is thus placed on candidates not only to obtain all the necessary training, but also to do it in a limited time frame. A certain amount of additional experience is also required, such as pastoring, teaching, farming, or working in a hospital. Between the time of the initial vocation and the submission of the application a number of years may pass—which can result in discouragement, insecurity, or loss of self-confidence.

Older, experienced candidates usually have their roots in an American, comfort-oriented lifestyle. Excitement about living and working in a totally different culture may be short-lived if it isn't followed by a genuine love for the people the missionary is working with. (See chapter 5, "The Letdown.")

What type of person is most likely to be a successful missionary? Each mission board has its own criteria, which may or may

**CHAPTER
1**

**The
Pedestal**

not be written policy. An important study on the prediction of missionary success through pretraining variables conducted by William G. Britt notes the following: More controlled, less moody, and more astute candidates tended to become better adjusted missionaries. Firstborn, younger candidates as well as those who scored high on perseverance and flexibility also adapted more easily. An important conclusion of this study was that the history of behavior was the best predictor of future behavior; although God's call and motivation were important factors, past experiences were more important in predicting how one would adjust to the stress of another culture. Other important factors were adaptability and interpersonal relationships. An interesting and unexpected result was that passive, accommodating candidates who responded to more authoritarian supervisors tended to be less successful overseas. This would seem to indicate that more aggressive candidates, who may tend to cause more conflict, became in the long run more successful missionaries.[5]

ORIENTATION

Orientation programs are as varied as the mission societies who organize and implement them. They range from two weeks to several months, and the subjects taught are constantly being reviewed in light of their effectiveness. But the purpose of every program is to prepare candidates for a long, successful, rewarding overseas ministry that will result in the development and strengthening of a national church and the conversion and discipleship of those who do not know Christ as their personal Savior.

Lyman Reed lists the following as outcomes of effective training:

1. Missionaries will be in a better position to understand the peoples to whom they go with the gospel.
2. They will be better communicators in a cross-cultural situation.
3. They will be less ethnocentric and more appreciative of other cultures.
4. Fewer of them will drop out.
5. They will have a more effective church-planting ministry.
6. They will more effectively help train their fellow missionaries.[6]

There are two basic types of orientation programs: experience-oriented, where the candidates receive hands-on training, and content-oriented, where the emphasis is placed on disseminating the greatest possible amount of information. Several missions organizations are now using a combination of the two and have seen a significant reduction in attrition.[7]

William Gundykunst, Mitchell Hammer, and Richard Wiseman suggest three areas that need to be incorporated into any cross-cultural training program:

1. Perspective training, concentrating on developing an intercultural perspective using the cultural self-awareness approach
2. Interaction training, involvement and interaction with people from the host country
3. Context specific training, focusing specifically on the particular situation the trainee will face in the host country.[8]

The size of the group of candidates and the nature of the work they are being trained for play an important role in the nature of the program. One organization that specializes in translating the Bible or portions of it into little known languages uses a boot camp approach to orientation.[9] The candidates live for several weeks under much the same conditions they will face when overseas. The camp is located in a wilderness area where there is no electricity or running water. The candidates are trained for living in a primitive village situation since most of them will face such conditions in the ministry. There is a strong bonding between the candidates as they share hardships and frustrations. As a result, culture shock is reduced when they arrive on the field.

This type of orientation is not suitable for a large group of candidates who will live under greatly diversified conditions and work in a variety of ministries. For example, an experiential program for candidates preparing for seminary teaching in Tokyo could not be the same as for candidates going to plant churches among a remote Indian tribe in the Andes. Such training ideally needs to be done on the field (although few mission boards have such programs).[10]

A study was conducted to determine if there are trait differences between successful missionaries working in different cultures. The factors examined were social skills, personal energy, outspokenness, and timidity. The results of the study showed that no single personality profile is ideal for all overseas assignments. Different situations vary significantly in what they demand of the missionary. The study suggests that the training of candidates should be specific to the culture and ministry demands of their area. Knowing these demands will enable them to select the ministries that are most consistent with their own preference, personalities, and style.[11]

Adrian Furnham and Stephen Bochner have proposed a system for dealing with culture shock that they call culture-based "social-skills training." They feel that most of the problems encountered by culture-learners involve interpersonal encounters with host members. "Consequently, a high priority is to identify those social situations that sojourners find particularly difficult, and then teach them the requisite culturally relevant social skills to enable these situations to be more effectively negotiated."[12] Although the authors were mainly interested in the culture shock experienced by businessmen and tourists, many of their principles could be used for missionaries.

Effective orientation continues throughout and beyond the first term of service. On-field orientation ranges from nonexistent to intense, depending on the field and mission board policy. Ronald Iwasko suggests a forty-hour program, which treats the following questions:

1. How do I relate to the [home office]?
2. How can I manage daily living requirements?
3. How can I care for my family?
4. What ministry skills do I need?
5. How can I become effective in the new culture?
6. How should I relate to other missionaries?
7. How should I relate to the national church?
8. How should I react to non-Christian philosophies, practices, and forces?[13]

The visit of a full-time, qualified counselor with missionary experience sometime during the first year on the field has been recommended as a method of reducing first-term dropouts.[14] The counselor would have all the privileges of that office in the States, would not be part of administration, and would have the authority to make recommended changes in placement and assignments, if necessary. Seeing firsthand the adjustment problems facing the new missionaries would help the counselor make suggestions for behavior modification or attitude change. Several organizations have full-time psychologists or psychiatrists on their staff who are used in the selection of candidates and the debriefing after each term. However, few of them seem to be utilized for regularly visiting missionaries on the field.

CHAPTER
1
———
The
Pedestal

INDOCTRINATION

Whereas orientation focuses on what the candidate will be doing, indoctrination focuses on what the missionary candidate will be teaching. If the candidate has had training in a denominational institution, the basic theological doctrines of the denomination have already been learned. However, if the candidate has attended a secular or nondenominational college or Bible institute, the mission board will need to ensure that the denomination's biblical beliefs will be proclaimed.

Because many evangelical sending organizations today are nondenominational, the indoctrination process becomes more complicated. Certain basic doctrines are generally stated (those adhered to by the majority of evangelical churches) and the candidates are asked to teach them and no others. But candidates, coming as they do from a wide range of churches, sometimes find it difficult to limit their teaching to these doctrines, especially if they have strong convictions that they are not permitted to express. This can be particularly true of charismatic candidates affiliated with noncharismatic organizations.

Another phenomenon on the field is the breakdown of divisions between many denominations. Where Christians are a very small minority, the biggest distinction comes between Catholics and Protestants, not between Baptists, Methodists, or Pentecostals, and in Muslim countries, Catholics and Protestants often come together. Although no statistics are available, cooperative evangelical outreaches, including large campaigns such as those conducted by Billy Graham, have taken place in many countries.

FINANCING

There are two major plans for missionary financing: one where the sending agency provides all necessary funds and the other where the missionary candidates raise their support by visiting churches and presenting the need, generally called "deputation." Most conciliar Protestant churches, such as the Methodists, Lutherans, and Presbyterians, provide all the financing for their missionaries, including funding for major projects. While on furlough, missionaries are asked to visit a number of churches to give a report on the progress of their work but are not under pressure to raise funds.

Among evangelical churches, the Southern Baptist organization also funds all missionaries who are salaried as soon as they are appointed.[15] Missionaries are still expected to visit a number of churches during furlough as well as attend church camps and mission conferences.

Each system has advantages and disadvantages. D. Kurt Nelson has suggested the following as advantages of the deputation system.

1. Deputation results in a broader prayer base.
2. It stretches the faith of missionary candidates as they depend upon God, over a lengthy period, to provide for their needed support.
3. It broadens the base of financial support and protects the missionary against losing significant support should one church fail to maintain the support.
4. It is an effective means of stimulating and encouraging the missionary vision of many smaller churches through increasing their exposure to many different missionaries and fields.[16]

A survey of 472 furlough missionaries affiliated with fifteen different agencies showed that the pressures and controversies of having to raise support and project funds was still a "boiling-point issue" for a substantial number.[17] As the cost of supporting missionaries increases (because of inflated living expenses overseas), the competition for church mission funds becomes keener. If the sending board provides all missionary finances, often through a tax system on all the churches in the denomination, they know exactly how many missionaries and projects they can fund.

Sending agencies who rely on candidates and furlough missionaries to raise the necessary funds generally do not try to limit the number of applicants. If the agency is affiliated with a denomination, then candidates and missionaries are competing for available funds in those churches. More personable, talented speakers will usually be able to raise the necessary funds, whether or not they have a ministry on the field that is more effective than that of the less personable missionary. Candidates applying to nondenominational or interdenominational agencies often find themselves competing for funds in churches not affiliated with any denomination. They may find themselves with the same dilemma.

New candidates are often put in the position of having to raise a budget within a limited amount of time, which greatly increases the pressure during deputation. Helen Herndon feels that missionaries who leave because of lack of funds have been "pushed out" because no church or board is willing to be financially responsible for them. She decries the often used phrase "Trust the Lord for your needs," believing it shows irresponsibility on the part of these agencies.[18] No pastor would serve a church unless it was willing to be financially responsible for him or her.

Added to the pressure to raise the stipulated funds in a limited amount of time is the "tin-cup" image. The son of one veteran missionary couple, when preparing to raise funds for a short-term assignment overseas, said, "I feel like a beggar!" Daniel Bacon contends that this image has become a major barrier to many young people contemplating career missions. He feels that this image can be dispelled when churches are taught a correct biblical perspective of missions. The missionary has the prophetic function of keeping the evangelistic task before the churches he or she is in partnership with. And partnership goes beyond finances, to mobilizing prayer and personnel. Interdependence, accountability, and reporting should result from this joint relationship.[19]

Nelson suggests several alternatives to traditional deputation. One method is for one church to pledge a significant amount of a missionary's support, 30 to 60 percent. Thus the missionary would be responsible to only a few churches. Similar to this is the consortium approach, where several churches team up to provide the total support needed. The missionary is usually a member of one of the churches and ministers in that church during furlough. And, finally, in the sending-church concept, one church supplies 80 to 90 percent of needed support, the balance being raised from individuals or family members. The sending church would "adopt" the missionary family, ministering to all their needs both overseas and on furlough.[20]

Since many mission boards are looking for overseas personnel today, candidates have options. They can closely review the policies of a number of agencies before making a decision. Herndon says that boards should be willing to be scrutinized just as they scrutinize candidates.[21]

---

[1]Harold W. Bernard and Wesley C. Huckins, *Dynamics of Personal Adjustment*, 2d ed. (Boston: Holbrook Press, 1975), 137.

[2]Carl R. Rogers, "The Concept of the Fully Functioning Person," *Psychotherapy* 1 (1963): 17–26.

[3]Bernard and Huckins, *Dynamics*, 172.

[4]Rev. Keith Parks, Director of Missions, Southern Baptist Convention, Richmond, Va., interviewed by Marge Jones, 1991.

[5]William Gordon Britt III, "Pretraining Variables in the Prediction of Missionary Success Overseas," *Journal of Psychology and Theology* 11 (Fall 1983): 203–12.

[6]Lyman E. Reed, *Preparing Missionaries for Intercultural Communication: A Bicultural Approach* (Pasadena, Calif.: William Carey Library, l985), 181–82.

[7]Summary of Roy S. Rosedale, "Cross-Cultural Missionary Training; Biblical Basis and Model" (Ph.D. diss., California Graduate School of Theology, 1981).

[8]William B. Gundykunst, Mitchell R. Hammer, and Richard L. Wiseman, "An Analysis of an Integrated Approach to Cross-Cultural Training," *International Journal of Intercultural Relations* 1 (Spring 1977): 107–8.

[9]Wycliffe Bible Translators.

[10]Ronald A. Iwasko, "An Integrated Program for Training First-Term Missionaries of the Assemblies of God" (D.Miss. diss., Trinity Evangelical Divinity School, 1984), 269–72.

[11]George M. Diekhoff et al., "The Ideal Overseas Missionary: A Cross-Cultural Comparison," *Journal of Psychology and Theology* 19 (Summer 1991): 178–85.

[12]Adrian Furnham and Stephen Bochner, *Culture Shock: Psychological Reactions to Unfamiliar Environments* (London: Methuen, 1986), 236, 243.

[13]Iwasko, "An Integrated Program," 269–72.

[14]Marge Jones, "First-Year Counseling: A Key Ingredient to Success," *Evangelical Missions Quarterly* 29 (July 1993): 294–97.

[15]Rev. Keith Parks, Director of Missions, Southern Baptist Convention, Richmond, Va., interviewed by Marge Jones, 1991.

[16]D. Kurt Nelson, "There Are Some Workable Alternatives to the Old Way of Doing Deputation," *Evangelical Missions Quarterly* 15 (October 1986): 365–71.

[17]Robert T. Coote, "A Boon or a 'Drag'? How North American Evangelical Missionaries Experience Home Furloughs," *International Bulletin of Missionary Research* 15 (January 1991): 17–23.

[18]Helen Louise Herndon, "How Many 'Dropouts' Really Are 'Pushouts'?" *Evangelical Missions Quarterly* 16 (January 1980): 13–15.

[19]Daniel W. Bacon, "The Tin-Cup Image Can Be Shattered," *Evangelical Missions Quarterly* 22 (October 1986): 376–78.

[20]Nelson, "Workable Alternatives," 365–71.

[21]Herndon, "How Many 'Dropouts,'" 13–15.

Chapter Two

The Rupture

OUT OF THE WOMB

Much has been written about the shock experienced by a newborn during the birth process. Hospitals and doctors in developed countries now do everything possible to lessen the shock, preparing an environment outside the womb that will duplicate as much as possible the situation inside the womb. A caring, loving support system of parents and medical personnel attends to the child's every need. The baby has only to cry and its physical and emotional needs are met.

Going to the field is an out-of-the-womb experience for most first-term missionaries. They have left the support system of family, friends, and church for an unknown, often hostile, environment. The expectation of a loving, caring support system is seldom realized. Local missionaries are usually busy with their responsibilities. Nationals in the church would like to provide the necessary support, but lack an understanding of the kind needed because they have a different value system. New missionaries will almost invariably seek to bond with someone from their own culture and socioeconomic status, whether inside or outside the mission family.

Adrian Furnham and Stephen Bochner state that the amount of shock experienced is directly proportional to the qualitative and quantitative differences in the value systems between a person's country of departure and the host country. To cope with the stress, the individual will try to create an atmosphere as close to the "womb" as possible. Marjory Foyle suggests that new missionaries pack one or two suitcases with familiar articles and toys that can be immediately put in prominent places in the host environment to make it look more like the home they left.[1]

G. Collins identifies nine sources of stress, most of which are experienced during a missionary's first term on the field:

1. Loneliness
2. Pressure of adjusting to a foreign culture
3. Constant demands on one's time
4. Lack of adequate medical facilities
5. Overwhelming workload and difficult working conditions
6. Pressure to be a constant, positive witness to nationals
7. Confusion over one's role within the local church
8. Frequent lack of privacy
9. Inability to get away for recreation and vacation[2]

A distinction needs to be made, however, between stress and anxiety. Myron Loss notes that stress comes from external pressures exerted on an individual by family, employers, friends, society, and religion. The internal tension that results from trying to live up to these pressures is anxiety. A certain amount of stress is necessary for motivation, but excessive stress can cause emotional and physical illness. Its effect varies from person to person, each having a different tolerance level for stress and one's own idiosyncratic way of responding.[3] In addition, the way a person perceives the stressful situation greatly affects the results of the stress on that person. The experience of change and adaptation to new conditions that cause stress may also be possible causes of ill health. The greater the change, the more likely one is to experience, or become vulnerable to, illness.[4]

Frances White notes two basic types of separation: (1) those considered developmental, which occur naturally as a person progresses from infancy to old age, and (2) those that are traumatic or unexpected. Developmental separations involve leaving behind old sources of gratification to develop more age-appropriate ways of need fulfillment and self-perception. Traumatic changes such as geographic moves, illnesses, job

**CHAPTER
2**

**The
Rupture**

changes, accidents, and disasters often cause multiple separations and losses. Missionaries experience not only the normal developmental separations but also, because of the nature of their work, an unusual number of situational changes.[5]

Frances White and Elaine Nesbit delineate four stages a person proceeds through after experiencing change, separation, or loss.

The first stage is denial. During this time the person makes a concerted effort to minimize the loss by writing often and promising to return home for important events. The missionary may even admire the scenery and people of the host culture, acting almost as though he or she were on vacation rather than adapting to a new residence.

The second stage is characterized by anger. This is expressed in impatience, gruffness, silence, or criticism, especially with friends and family.

The third stage of separation is sadness. This surfaces when a person recognizes the reality of the separation that has caused the loss. White refers to this stage as the affective phase, when depression and a sense of despair may be present. The individual may also feel anger and guilt because of the ambivalence that is part of any meaningful relationship.

The final stage is resolution. This involves accepting and adjusting to the new culture positively. The person accepts the loss, allowing integration of the new situation into his or her life, and begins to live in the present. Resolution permits the incorporation of parts of the former life into the new.[6]

Having secure attachments to primary caregivers is a necessary ingredient for healthy development. The baby's attachment to the mother starts in the first few months. This lays the foundation upon which the child develops. Babies experience tremendous distress when this attachment is disrupted. When new missionaries leave the "womb" they leave their attachments, which results in a feeling of loss, as well as other emotions, until new attachments are made. White points out that field leaders need to consider the importance of attachment figures when placing missionaries, taking into consideration which personality types are compatible.[7] Several missions now use teams where individuals work together to accomplish specific tasks.[8] These teams may consist of couples or couples and singles, each person using his or her area of expertise to accomplish a common goal.

One mission board permits some of their younger candidates to do their ministerial training overseas.[9] They are assigned to a senior missionary on the field and work directly under his or her supervision, with regular reports sent to the home office. This system provides an immediate attachment figure for the individual or couple while they adjust to the new culture. During an earlier generation, new missionaries were rarely sent to work alone on any field. After the Second World War, when missionaries again flocked to overseas assignments, the terms "senior missionary" and "junior missionary" were seldom used. But the concept of support from an experienced missionary was still often very important. There may have been a number of difficulties inherent in the senior-junior program, but there was also the possibility of firm, positive, long-term attachments.

Some mission boards do not permit single women missionaries to work alone. When their female companion is a compatible person with the same interests and lifestyle, an important attachment can be made that can help the individuals through difficult situations. In a remote area in the interior of Africa, living conditions were so difficult that a number of families left after only one term. However, two single female nurses continued to minister for many years together. The support they gave each other because of healthy attachment helped them through seemingly impossible hardships. Each bolstered the other's sense of humor, which enabled them to laugh at each other as well as at the situation.

Separations that have been successfully accepted can make a person more mature, achieving a healthy, differentiated self. Otherwise, a person may experience "anxious separation," causing excessive attachments or an avoidance of close bonding. White suggests that a trained professional make family evaluations of all missionary candidates with respect to their tolerance for varying degrees of togetherness-closeness and separation-differentiation. She feels that the higher the tolerance, the freer the family members are to experience a healthy balance of dependence and independence. The evaluation should examine the parents' separation from their families of origin as well as the quality of their present relationships with extended family and friends. "The more mental health professionals can diagnose intimacy problems and offer appropriate help to missionaries before they go to the field, the more positive could be their relationships to others."[10]

Missionaries who have formed unhealthy relationships with parents tend to bring those faulty relationships to the field. They may cause them to make subtle demands for allegiance from coworkers or nationals. One missionary caused serious disruptive problems in the national church because of an unhealthy attachment to his mother, which probably could have been diagnosed while he was a candidate. After he had been dismissed from missionary service, his wife revealed that he wrote to his mother daily and kept all her letters, tied in bundles with ribbons, hidden in an office drawer.

He had formed a very close attachment to the national church president, who lived on the same mission compound, helping him obtain dairy cattle and poultry. The missionary, through his contacts, sold his and the president's produce to hotel and restaurant owners in a nearby city, using mission vehicles for transport. This caused serious division between the president and the pastors he was responsible to. Even though the missionary's credentials were withdrawn by the denomination, he continued to make regular trips to visit the president, constantly helping him to upgrade his farm. He even made arrangements for the president to come to America for a visit. The ex-missionary eventually divorced his wife, spending more and more time with the president right up to the ex-missionary's reportedly suicidal death.

White also suggests that psychoeducative seminars could be an effective means of helping candidates recognize and prepare for the separation process. They should be designed to help missionaries understand the normal separation process, identify the stages, and learn to be comfortable talking with each other about their reactions to separations, thus defusing the effects of leave-taking. The family will also better understand hostile or withdrawn behaviors, which may accompany separation, and feel less guilty or rejected.[11]

A number of conditions the candidate may face on the mission field can aggravate the out-of-the-womb experience. The author found the following experiences to be some of the most traumatic for first-term missionaries.

**CHAPTER
2**

**The
Rupture**

An educated African woman was asked, after visiting the States, what impressed her the most about America. "There are no burglar bars on your windows or doors" was her unequivocal reply. Apart from those living in large cities, most Americans feel relatively secure in their homes and neighborhoods. Children ride buses to school without soldiers to guard them, and they play outdoors when school is not in session. Adults walk or jog along quiet streets or in parks without fear. Driving to the grocery store or mall for shopping does not entail being stopped by the police unless there has been a traffic violation. Most Americans believe that people are basically good, kind, and helpful, that the police force and judicial system are basically honest and can be relied upon when needed.

Much of this changes when missionaries arrive on their assigned fields. The security system is gone. In many third world countries, every door and window is secured with iron burglar bars and houses are surrounded by security fences or walls. Frequently, neither the police force nor the judicial system can be relied on for justice, and the police force may even be a source of stress rather than a source of security. Corruption is often an accepted way of life.

Upon facing the reality that there is no longer a security system, one may experience a variety of reactions. In extreme cases, the missionary may refuse to leave the house except for trips to church, the place of service, or the residence of a known acquaintance. Wives refuse to go shopping alone and to drive the car. Children are not allowed to play with the local children. All family activity is confined to the home; there is no interaction with the local people or culture.

One missionary family arrived on the field with several drums of reading material and videos for the children, who were home schooled. Although the husband spent a great deal of time ministering in village churches, where he lived with his hosts, his wife and children stayed behind the walls surrounding the mission house. Even though they lived in a small rural town where there was little or no danger from local inhabitants, the children were not permitted outside the walls unless accompanied by a parent. Instead of spending quality time investigating their new environment and bonding with peers in their host country, the children spent all their time reading novels and watching videos, which their father had edited.

If a successful transition is to occur, accepting the reality that little or no local security system exists and coping with the resultant stress require a change in attitude on the part of most new missionaries. They will need to learn to deal with the situation the same way the local population does. Generally, the best source of help is the local church leadership. Making the right government connections is also important, such as becoming acquainted with the police chief or customs agent. If other mission societies are already established in the area, they too can be a source of information and help.

SAFETY TO DANGER

Missionaries going to danger-zone countries to minister are generally given special psychological and physical training before being sent. They expect constant bomb scares and gunfire. Families are usually left in safe areas with adequate protection. Every facet of their lives is controlled by the situation, which they accept as the norm.

Very few new missionaries are sent to minister in danger-zone countries. They do not expect to face danger every time they step out the door. However, in many third world countries, living in danger is the normal way of life. Locked cars can be opened in seconds. Thievery is endemic. Gangs roam the streets at night with guns. Encounters with hostile soldiers are an everyday occurrence. Government coups, riots, and revolutions can occur at any time. Jewelry, watches, and purses are snatched in daylight on main streets. Anything that isn't nailed down or locked up could disappear.

One family went through a very traumatic experience as they watched people being killed across the street from their home. The security guards of a former government leader who had been voted out in democratic elections had a gun battle with government agents over the course of several days. The sight of these dead and wounded men made an indelible impression on the wife, causing an anxiety for her family that could not be soon forgotten.

Lack of adequate medical help is often a constant source of anxiety. Although emergency medical equipment is kept in the home and first-aid training is given during orientation, accidents can occur at any time that cannot be handled by family members. Missionaries need to have a well-thought-out and prepared plan for medical emergencies. Where possible, contact should be made with support agencies who are prepared to evacuate emergency cases by air.

SUPPORT SYSTEM TO SELF-RELIANCE

Few people living in the United States are cognizant of the number of support systems they can access. Family members can be reached for help at the touch of a button. Close friends can be called any time of the day or night. Pastoral care is an integral part of church membership. Decisions are made after consulting experts. Appliance, house, and car repairs are generally made by qualified, competent personnel who guarantee their work.

Few, if any, of these support systems exist on many mission fields. The missionary finds that he or she has the sole responsibility for all decisions. Maintenance personnel consists of the missionary family in many areas. This is also true of spiritual and psychological help. The missionary who does not have or cannot develop a high level of self-reliance will have difficulty adjusting to the new life.

COMFORT TO INCONVENIENCE

The whole economic system in the United States functions for the comfort of the individual. The customer is always right. Drive-up windows are provided not only by eating places but also by banks, mortgage companies, grocery stores, and hardware outlets. A comfortable home and car are taken for granted. Bills can be paid by check or credit card. Shopping can be done over the telephone and deliveries made to the house, including daily mail service. Important letters and packages can be sent overnight. Prompt, efficient service is an integral part of company policies.

What coping mechanism is available to the missionary when faced with a situation where nothing functions for the comfort of the individual or, as in some cases, nothing functions at all? Telephone service, if available, is slow, irregular, and/or very expensive. Service is very low on priority lists. Mail service is unreliable. Well-organized bank scams operate through the postal service. Banks take three weeks to three months to cash checks. Paying a utility bill usually takes all morning. The normal waiting time for food in a restaurant is an hour. Finding a simple hardware item often means visiting a dozen stores.

Frustration sets in because so much time and energy are spent in the ordinary tasks of living that the missionary has little left for the ministry. Questions such as Why am I here? are ever present in the individual's mind. Lesson and sermon preparation time is relegated to early morning or late evening hours. Unless special steps are taken, family time disappears and fourteen-hour workdays become the norm.

KNOWN TO UNKNOWN

Arriving on the mission field, an adult suddenly becomes like a child again. All the knowledge he or she has gained is of little or no value. Because of language differences, even the most educated cannot express themselves or understand the simplest instructions. Social structures are an unknown maze. Appropriate conduct for each individual situation has to be learned.

In addition, the value system of the host country is completely different. What had been considered a lie is no longer a lie; truth is relative instead of absolute. The line between stealing and borrowing becomes very faint when hunger is a way of life. A bribe suddenly becomes a "tip" when realization dawns that nothing will be accomplished without accommodation to the system.

Goal-oriented Americans suddenly find themselves in a people-oriented society. Relationships are far more important than getting the job done. Goal setting causes consternation and frustration. Hours of "talk" time have to be programmed into each day's activities.

The missionary is also confronted with an entirely different worldview. To begin with, no matter how little the missionary's living allowance, he or she is considered rich because "all Americans are rich." In many cases, socialism is much preferred to democracy by the people and multiparty systems promote tribalism. The quickest way to become persona non grata is to become involved in politics. Honesty is no longer the best public or private policy and self-expression can easily lead to expulsion.

LOVE TO HOSTILITY

"Love one another" is not just a Christian ideal in the United States. It is an intrinsic part of the culture. Bumper stickers with hearts can be found on any street in any city. Altruism is taught in schools and preached from every pulpit. Sentiments are to be expressed in kind deeds and not in hostile acts, which will be rewarded with punishment. Hostile children and adults alike are shunned.

The motivation for missions is love. Missionaries are ready to face the rupture because of love. They want, expect, and try to love those they will be working with. They also expect that their effort will be rewarded with reciprocal feelings of acceptance, if not love. However, in many cases, they will be met with feelings of hostility instead of acceptance. "Yankee go home" is an often expressed attitude. They are not disliked or rejected as an individual but because of the group they represent: American, Christian, missionary.

How will the missionary react when rocks are thrown at the house or car or when spit upon? Love cannot be conveyed by words and the necessary actions become very difficult. Praying for enemies becomes a daily routine. Establishing a working relationship with someone who is doing everything possible to thwart the work the missionary is doing can become a challenge or a threat.

Loss states that "[t]he most devastating result of cross-cultural conflict is not a state of shock. Rather, it is a slowly advancing, nearly unnoticed psychological phenomenon which affects [a person's] whole way of thinking about himself and about others." The early experience of fascination for the culture is replaced by dissatisfaction with the inconveniences, which eventually ends in one of four responses:

1. total rejection of the new culture
2. total rejection of the old culture
3. grudging coexistence
4. healthy integration of the new with the old[12]

White and Nesbit list three unhealthy reactions to what they call change, separation, and loss.

1. Suppressing emotions, which causes relationships to devel-

op slowly or remain on a superficial level. Suppressed emotions by parents can affect the emotional growth in children.

2. Remaining in one stage of the process (denial, anger, sadness, resolution).

3. Being unable to form new and deep relationships or to make commitments. Although working in a foreign country, mentally the individual is still living at home.

White and Nesbit give the following suggestions to help with separation:

1. Talk with others about feelings.
2. Listen carefully to family members.
3. Have farewell and welcome gatherings, which help with transitions.
4. Don't be afraid to form new attachments.
5. Create as much sameness and predictability as possible for the family.
6. Allow family members time to adjust and express negative feelings.[13]

A number of positive steps can be taken by new missionaries to help in the adjustment process after the rupture. This author suggests the following:

1. Recognize what is happening; realize that a rupture is taking place.
2. Accept negative responses as normal.
3. Talk out and pray through negative responses.
4. Select positive actions to offset or overcome negative responses.
5. Don't expect immediate bonding.
6. Remember the reason for being on the mission field.
7. Keep a good sense of humor. Learn to laugh at mistakes.

To positively adjust to the rupture experience, new missionaries are probably going to have to make what Laura Gardner calls a "transformational shift." This is an attitudinal, volitional, conscious shift in their values, presuppositions, and coping devices to be able to contend with the dissonance and still have energy left for productive ministry.[14] In other words, they will need to learn to look at every situation through the eyes of their host country neighbors. They will need to consciously replace old mind-sets (ways of thinking and reacting) with new ones, permitting innovative solutions to seemingly impossible circumstances.

[1]Adrian Furnham and Stephen Bochner, *Culture Shock: Psychological Reactions to Unfamiliar Environments* (London: Methuen, 1986), 189; Marjory F. Foyle, *Overcoming Missionary Stress* (Wheaton, Ill.: Evangelical Missions Information Service, 1987), 55.

[2]Summary of G. Collins, *You Can Profit from Stress* (Santa Ana, Calif.: Vision House, 1977).

[3]Myron Loss, *Culture Shock: Dealing with Stress in Cross-Cultural Living* (Winona Lake, Ind.: Light and Life Press, 1983), 11–23.

[4]Furnham and Bochner, *Culture Shock*, 181.

[5]Frances J. White, "Some Reflections on the Separation Phenomenon Idiosyncratic to the Experience of Missionaries and Their Children," *Journal of Psychology and Theology* 11 (Fall 1983): 181–88.

[6]Frances J. White and Elaine M. Nesbit, "Separation: Balancing the Gains and Losses," *Evangelical Missions Quarterly* 22 (October 1986): 392–98.

[7]White, "Some Reflections," 181–88.

[8]One organization that uses the group approach is Mission: Moving Mountains, P. O. Box 1168, Burnsville, MN 55337-0168.

[9]The Missionary-in-Training program of the Division of Foreign Missions of the Assemblies of God, Springfield, Mo.

[10]White, "Some Reflections," 181–88.

[11]Ibid.

[12]Loss, *Culture Shock*, 57–58.

[13]White and Nesbit, "Separation," 392–98.

[14]Laura Mae Gardner, "Proactive Care of Missionary Personnel," *Journal of Psychology and Theology* 15 (Winter 1987): 308–14.

Chapter Three

The Language Grind

Learning the language of the host country is often the first developmental task new missionaries face. Being suddenly thrust into a situation where they are complete outsiders, where they cannot communicate, can be a shock to their psychological stability. They have lost an ingredient that gave them status and security. No matter how well educated, they now feel like an idiot. They no longer have the ability to give an answer to the simplest question.

Most missionary candidates have had an active and productive ministry in their field, whether religious or secular, before applying for appointment. Their ability to express their knowledge, in written or verbal form, was an integral part of their feeling of self-worth. Language is the primary ingredient in interpersonal relationships and this ingredient has suddenly been removed. Learned knowledge cannot be shared, active ministry has come to a standstill, productivity is at its lowest point. As a new missionary who had a doctorate in administration remarked while studying French in Switzerland, "You get on a bus. The fellow sitting next to you, well dressed and intelligent looking, opens his mouth and sounds like an idiot."

Donald Larson, who has done extensive research on the problems inherent in learning a foreign language, notes that cross-cultural communicative skills come from competency in the language of the host country. Before the candidates can acquire a new language, they need to understand where they have come from and what has made them what they are. He calls this "exit orientation." They also need "entry orientation," which helps them see what they have to do to meet their own expectations as well as those of others in their host country.

He refers to the person learning a new language as an outsider, a nonmember of the group, a nonuser of the local language, and a nonbearer of the local culture. Overtly or covertly, the person is treated as unacceptable. Larson mentions two diseases that affect the language learner:

1. "monolingual myopia": a disease of the tongue which affects the vision—we see people better when we can talk their language.
2. "lathophobic aphasia": failure to speak for fear of making a mistake.[1]

The learner is caught in a web of conflicting expectations, his own expectations, the expectations of the people whose language he is studying, the expectations of his fellow learners, and the expectations of the home office. He realizes he will be living an unsettled life, will never be able to adapt to the culture of the local people, nor have a satisfying ministry until he can understand and express himself adequately in the local language. The hours, days, weeks, months, and sometimes years of constant mental struggle to memorize vocabulary, verb forms, foreign expressions, strange sounds and hard-to-distinguish tones, not to mention a totally different alphabet, could take a heavy physical and emotional toll.[2] "Is this really worth the effort when I will probably never be fluent and can always use an interpreter?" The person may come to the decision that he or she doesn't have the mental capacity to learn the language and stop making an effort.

Another decision on the part of the learner may be that a rudimentary knowledge of the language is all that is necessary, since the local population does not expect him to be fluent. He has enough of the language to understand most conversations and to make himself understood, but for ministry, preaching or teaching, he will use an interpreter who is much more able to communicate his thoughts in the local language. This is often the case with missionaries who have transferred from one field to another where they can no longer use the language first learned.

When a number of candidates attend the same language school, keen competition often results, putting an undue pressure on the slower learner. Although repeating a level would be the best solution to learning basic grammar, the learner will feel obligated to keep up with the others who started at the same time. Also, the mission board may have a time limit for attending language school that presupposes going from one level to the next with no repeats.

There is also the pressure to keep up with one's spouse, even if the spouse has a much greater natural ability to learn a language. Definite feelings of frustration and inadequacies can result, especially if the wife is able to learn the language more easily than the husband. Spending extra time in language study so that the slower learner can come up to the standard of the quicker learner should be a priority. Unfortunately, in many cases, the wife, who has the responsibility of taking care of children and home as well as studying the language, is not given the extra time needed to reach the level of communicative skill of her husband. Not only will her ministry be limited on the field but she may well harbor resentment because of what she considers discrimination.

Some mission boards not only set time limits for language study but also specify proficiency levels. Those candidates not able to meet these standards are forced to consider working in the home office, returning to ministry in the States, or going to a country where English can be used. If a candidate has felt a call to a specific people group and then finds himself unable to master the language required to communicate with them, doubt about God's call may well arise or feelings of failing to measure up to God's will. In either case, one's self-worth will have suffered.

Most mission boards now use a language aptitude test for all their candidates, such as the Modern Language Aptitude Test, Form A.[3] Although these tests show inherent ability to understand the basic structure of language, they cannot adequately indicate a person's tenacity, determination, or study habits. In one case, the wife scored the highest mark in the class on the aptitude test while her husband, a foreign national who became a naturalized American citizen, scored the lowest, even though he already spoke five languages fluently, including English. She went on to learn French, in which she ministers with competency, while he continues to learn new African languages within a few months, whenever necessary, to communicate with the people with whom they are working.

Counseling should be an integral part of language aptitude testing, especially for those with low scores, to help the candidates make appropriate choices for their future ministry. Their backgrounds as well as all the other factors involved in successful language learning should be seriously considered. Alternative areas of ministry where proficiency in a difficult language is not required should be proposed. Competency in a foreign language is only one part of successful missionary service. Many missionaries have communicated adequately with poor language skills and have had long and rewarding times of service, often much loved by the people they have been working with because of their love and concern.

There are certain factors that seem to contribute to successful language learning:

INHERENT ABILITY

Larson considers three factors important in language acquisition: the approach, the intensity, and the scope of skills or ability. He suggests that many people fail because they do not distinguish the difference between learning and studying. A person begins to learn a language by taking charge of those who already know it, family members or host people. A person studies a language by submitting to the control of teachers. Language is learned from those who know it and is studied under teachers. The most effective way to become a communicator in a language is to be a learner who takes advantage of every opportunity to study.[4]

Infants and children learn languages by hearing them, by being constantly surrounded by sounds that eventually come to have certain meanings.[5] They understand the language being spoken to them long before they can articulate a reply, and they learn to articulate some sounds before others. In other words, even children find some communicatory sounds more difficult than others despite their hearing them all the time. Using the proper mouth, tongue, and lip formations takes time and effort.

Distinguishing between sounds that are very similar is also learned, which can be very difficult for an adult if the distinction was not made in his or her childhood language. There is no difference between the *l* and the *r* in many non-European languages and they are used interchangeably. Therefore the formation of these two sounds in the mouth has to be studied because the ear does not pick up the difference.

If it were possible for any adult to learn any new language with a high degree of competency, then there would be no need for language aptitude tests.

The fact remains that some people are much more adept at learning languages than their fellow students. Desire as well as technique certainly plays a part in learning a language. However, neither desire nor technique is going to help a person who is tone-deaf learn a tonal language. Nor is someone who has never developed effective study habits suddenly going to be able to effectively study a foreign language. Placing these people in such stressful situations may well cause mental and physical fatigue as well as emotional damage due to failure.[6]

Joan Rubin and Irene Thompson consider persistence as important as ability. A person with a high rating on language aptitude tests will probably obtain better grades in a classroom situation, especially where the emphasis is on grammar and memorization, but such tests do not measure the individual's ability to learn unconsciously and intuitively. Pronunciation accuracy in adults has been shown to depend on two factors: "aptitude for mimicry, presumably an inherent trait, and strength of concern for pronunciation, a motivational factor."[7]

PERSONALITY

Personality also seems to play an important part in the effort that will have to be expended to learn a new language. A person who is naturally an extrovert, who enjoys contact with others, whether strangers or acquaintances, will tend to use any means possible to communicate. Because such people enjoy talking, often just for the sake of talking, they will constantly use each new word or phrase as they learn it. They will not be inhibited by mistakes in grammar or pronunciation. Their enjoyment of understanding others coupled with the ability to communicate will give constant impetus to renewed effort in language learning. Their lack of inhibitions augments their ability to tolerate making mistakes, as well as to profit from the criticism of those who speak the language.

On the other hand, a shy, withdrawn person who prefers solitude may have difficulty using any language ability he or she might have. Extra emotional effort will be needed to make the necessary contacts to use his or her language skills. This type of person can be devastated by criticism or by making mistakes and may well stop language study if placed in highly competitive classroom situations.[8] Not only the intellectual capacity but also the emotional effort needed to succeed may cause the candidate to withdraw from missionary service.

Some personality types consider any learning situation a challenge.[9] They approach a new language as a mountain to be conquered as quickly as possible. All effort is focused on attaining their goal—communicating effectively in a new situation. No distractions that might interfere with their single-minded purpose are tolerated. Generally such a person will learn the language well in a short time, often to the detriment of the rest of the family, which has had to sacrifice so that the member learning the language can obtain that goal. If the person is single, there are seldom any problems. But in a family situation, the needs of the wife and children often become secondary to the all-important need of the husband's preparation for the new ministry.

AGE

As Rubin and Thompson have pointed out, children do not learn a language better or more correctly than adults, because adults have better memories, more organized study habits, and greater motivation. Also they are more interested in correct grammar and the proper use of vocabulary. Children (under the age of fifteen) usually tend to have much better pronunciation because they learn through hearing, not seeing. They make friends more easily than adults and are generally not worried about making mistakes as long as they are communicating.[10]

Unfortunately, few missionary candidates have the privilege of learning in their childhood the language they will use as adults on the mission field. Although some missionary children do return as adult ministers to their parents' field of service, they are a small percentage of the total missionary force. Some mission boards are now looking to recruit as many ethnic Americans as possible to return to their, or their parents', country of origin, both because of the ability to learn a language which they either spoke or heard in the home and the ability to adjust to the culture of the country they are familiar with.

Therefore, the age differential which has to be considered is not between children and adults but between young adults and older adults. As noted before, missionary candidates today tend to be five to ten years older than those of twenty years ago. There seems to be a marked difference in the ability to learn any new subject when one is twenty-five or thirty-five, especially the subtle nuances of reading and writing as well as speaking a totally foreign language.[11]

Both Larson and Rubin and Thompson noted that motivation along with determination can be driving forces at any age to learn even the most complicated language.[12] However, mission boards are generally reluctant to send any candidate or veteran missionary over forty into a situation where a difficult language has to be learned. As there is little empirical data to indicate that age is a critical factor in determining language learning ability, mission boards must assess the candidate's intellectual capacity and attitude as well as his or her age. Positive attitudes about the people and culture usually help learners achieve language mastery. A pragmatic attitude about the need for mastery for career purposes can also help.

LOCATION AND TYPE

Donald Larson and William Smalley feel that the ideal location for learning a language is in the country where the candidate is going to minister, among the people who speak the language.[13] However, some languages, such as Spanish, French, and Portuguese, are spoken in a number of different countries and the ideal location may not be the one the missionary is going to. There are a number of specialized language schools established particularly for missionaries, where the specialized needs of foreign ministry are taken into consideration.[14]

In these schools there is generally a rather rigidly structured program, which the candidate needs to follow step by step. The instruction is geared to the class norm, with those having diffi-culty falling further and further behind. Sometimes, in an effort to encourage speaking skills, a rule is set that only the language being learned may be spoken in all public places after so many weeks. Fraternization with local people is encouraged. Special time is spent in learning theological language with time given in upper-level classes to prepare sermons or study notes. Also, the tuition is generally quite reasonable.

Although ideal for many candidates, there are several weak-nesses in the above conventional language school approach, noted by Lyman Reed.[15] The milieu is academic whereas lan-guage learning is a social activity. In most cases the teachers do the talking and the learners listen. Sometimes the schools are isolated from the community. Learners become totally involved with the techniques and mechanics of language study with little time for speaking. Often the emphasis is on teaching methods rather than learning methods. Teachers may be more interested in covering a set amount of material than in what the students are actually retaining. Reed's findings were applicable whether the school is especially geared for missionaries or for any foreign language student.

If the language school is located in a large city, generally some kind of international school in English is available for the candi-dates' children. There is always the question of whether the chil-dren should be placed in a local-language school or in a school where classes are taught in English. Preschool, kindergarten, and first-grade students can generally adapt to a local-language school situation. Older students can be traumatized if they are suddenly faced with learning new material in a language they do not understand. Some schools have special classes just to help foreign students acquire the language skills necessary to con-tinue their education in that language.

Older students will often fall back a year if they continue their education in a foreign language. In all cases, the needs of the children should be considered just as much as those of the parents. Deep-seated resentment can build up in children not only against the frustrating situation they find themselves in but also against their parents for putting them in such a situation.[16]

Another type of language study advocated by some mission boards is total immersion in a nonstructured setting. The candi-dates live with a national family and hear only the national language. They are forced to communicate to carry on daily living. The host family will do everything possible to help the candidates learn first simple vocabulary, then simple sentences, then more complicated thought patterns. The candidates are learning not only a language but also a culture. They are preparing themselves to live in a foreign situation as well as to communicate in a foreign language.

As Reed has pointed out, 65 percent of communication is nonverbal, received and sent through the senses without the use of language. Kinesic communication by means of gestures and body actions is seldom taught or learned in a formal setting. Only close contact with nationals over a continued period of time permits a person to learn not only to understand but also to effectively use this type of communication.[17]

Difficulties arise if the living standard of the host family causes physical and emotional problems for the candidates (see chapter 4). Also, most American learners are used to and need a structured setting. They need to know as much *about* the language as the language itself to feel that they have mastered one step before going on to the next. They prefer a logical progression to what may seem at first total confusion.

The ideal situation would be to combine structured and nonstructured language learning. Individual tutors are usually available along with classroom settings. Some students may prefer to rely completely on individual tutoring where they can learn at their own pace rather than the forced pace of a formal setting. They may be more apt to express themselves without the fear of being criticized or ridiculed. They can ask questions at any time and, when more advanced in the language, study specifically the vocabulary needed for their particular ministry.

There are also a number of self-instructional language courses available in major languages, which missionary candidates can use to good advantage before starting formal language classes.[18] Since these courses are often on cassette tapes, candidates can profit from hearing the sounds of the new language repeatedly while traveling during deputation. Even a very basic knowledge of the language, such as greetings or how to ask directions or order a meal in a restaurant, can greatly reduce the strain of adjustment on arrival in a strange setting.

Several major universities, such as the University of Michigan, offer summer courses in regional trade languages of the developing world. Many of these courses have been organized for Peace Corps and diplomatic personnel but are also open to anyone who may be interested. The Peace Corps has also organized short-term, intensive local and tribal language-learning centers, which, in many cases, are open to missionaries. However, during these courses the volunteers live as the nationals live, totally integrated into the local culture, speaking nothing but the local language. For single missionary candidates or couples without children who are able to take the pressure, this can be a very satisfactory method of learning the basics of a new language. Continued study, with a tutor if possible, will develop fluency and proficiency.

Because all missionary candidates have not come out of the same mold, it would seem that mission boards should have a flexible approach to language study. The candidates' special needs and abilities should be considered, as well as time and cost factors. This first major step in cross-cultural communication, which will have an important impact on the candidates' future ministry, needs to receive considerable attention.

---

[1]Summary of Donald N. Larson, *Guidelines for Barefoot Language Learning* (St. Paul, Minn.: CMS Publishing, 1984).

[2]Marjory F. Foyle, *Overcoming Missionary Stress* (Wheaton, Ill.: Evangelical Missions Information Service, 1987), 102–5.

[3]Psychological Corporation, 757 Third Ave., New York, NY 10017.

[4]Larson, *Guidelines*, 5–10.

[5]Donald N. Larson and William A. Smalley, *Becoming Bilingual: A Guide to Language Learning* (Pasadena, Calif.: William Carey Library, 1972), 7–20.

[6]Foyle, *Overcoming*, 103.

[7]Joan Rubin and Irene Thompson, *How to Be a More Successful Language Learner* (Boston: Heinle & Heinle Publishers, 1982), 5–11.

[8]Ibid., 6–11.

[9]For information on personality types see Nicholas S. DiCaprio, *Personality Theories: A Guide to Human Nature*, 2d ed. (New York: Holt, Rinehart and Winston, 1983).

[10]Rubin and Thompson, *Successful Language*, 4.

[11]Malcolm Knowles, *The Adult Learner: A Neglected Species*, 2d ed. (Houston, Tex.: Gulf Publishing, 1978), 158.

[12]Rubin and Thompson, *Successful Language*, 6.

[13]Larson and Smalley, *Becoming Bilingual*, 88–92.

[14]Two such schools are Institudo De Lengua Copanola in San Jose, Costa Rica, for learning Spanish and Association Francaise D'Enseignement Biblique in Albertville, France, for learning French.

[15]Lyman E. Reed, *Preparing Missionaries for Intercultural Communication: A Bicultural Approach* (Pasadena, Calif.: William Carey Library, 1985), 65–66.

[16]For information on parent/child stress see Foyle, *Overcoming*, chap. 4. Also note the bibliography for books on missionary children problems.

[17]Reed, *Preparing Missionaries*, 65–66.

[18]Berlitz and Barron are two of the better known companies that provide self-instructional language courses. More information can be obtained from the public library or from mission agencies.

Chapter Four

Bonding

If, as has been mentioned, the motivation for missions is love, the question remains, How can that love best be communicated in the host country? The Word must be communicated for the love of God shown through the death and resurrection of Christ to become a reality. Any number of books exist on communicating the gospel cross-culturally, for example, Lyman Reed's *Preparing Missionaries for Intercultural Communication: A Bicultural Approach.* But the process of communication comes as much from actions as from words. The dilemma for the missionary, then, is, How must I change my lifestyle in order for my actions to be perceived as an outgrowth of my love for the people I have come to reach?

Kalervo Oberg, an anthropologist, was the first person to use the term "culture shock." He names six aspects of this phenomenon:

1. Strain due to the effort required to make necessary psychological adaptations.

2. A sense of loss and feelings of deprivation in regard to friends, status, profession, and possessions.

3. Being rejected by and/or rejecting members of the new culture.

4. Confusion in role, role expectations, values, feelings, and self-identity.
5. Surprise, anxiety, even disgust and indignation, after becoming aware of cultural differences.
6. Feelings of impotence due to the inability to cope with the new environment.[1]

Most candidate orientation programs now treat the subject of culture shock in depth, as one of the important ingredients in the missionary's future adjustment in the host country. Probably all of the above feelings are discussed to prepare future missionaries for what they will be facing. But no amount of theory can take the place of reality. Marjory Foyle's simple explanation that culture shock is the reaction experienced on exchanging a familiar culture for an unfamiliar one is probably the most comprehensive.[2]

Harold Bernard and Wesley Huckins mention that a person must be able to explain and to make some sort of sense out of his or her surroundings to feel secure. However, understanding does not necessarily lead to acceptance. Nor does explanation necessarily lead to adaptation or integration. It is only natural for missionaries to be endowed with a large quantity of ethnocentrism—which, according to Lyman Reed, consists of viewing alien customs by applying the concepts and values of one's own culture.[3] In many parts of Africa as well as Asia, rats are considered a culinary delicacy, but new American missionaries would probably be hard-pressed to eat them. The dress codes in many Muslim countries could be considered sexist by modern American women but are accepted as decent, normal covering where they are worn.

Reed also observes that the danger of ethnocentrism is an attitude of superiority, which may then destroy personal relationships. A much more acceptable attitude would be that of cultural relativism: accepting all cultures as being equally valid in differing ways. Any aspect of a culture should be viewed only in relation to its own cultural context. To overcome ethnocentrism, the person should develop an attitude of mutual respect; build trust with words, actions, and thoughts; and accept others by spending quality time with members of the host country apart from church and professional events.

Until new missionaries can accept the values and customs of the host country as being as valid as their own, it will be difficult for bonding to begin. Reed suggests that for true bonding to take place, a missionary needs to become a bicultural, as opposed to a monocultural, person. This happens when the missionary learns (1) to accept others as they are even though they may be vastly different from the missionary, and (2) to feel at home in two or more cultures without undue stress or anxiety.[4]

Becoming bicultural takes a conscious effort on the part of the missionary. It means having informal associations with the host people apart from contacts made through ministry. Warm friendships with nationals can often break down a number of barriers associated with ethnocentrism. Many missionaries have found national dishes to be healthy and delicious after they become accustomed to the different flavors. They not only serve these dishes to nationals but also eat them as family meals. The wife of the director for Africa for a large evangelical denomination consistently prepares West African dishes for her company in America. She is known as an outstanding hostess who serves gourmet meals. Although food is only one part of breaking down ethnocentric barriers, it often plays a much greater part in third world socializing than in Western culture.

Another important factor is the use of time. American missionaries usually program their work by clocks and watches, whereas the host people may well be far more interested in what is happening and who is participating.[5] One missionary bought a partially finished house from a national doctor. The original living room faced the road where all the action was. However, when the mission house was finished, the living room was at the back of the house overlooking a beautiful river, making the nationals think the missionary was more concerned about the scenery than about them. Learning to be comfortable through three- and four-hour church services by being interested in the people and their needs is another part of becoming bicultural and is well worth the effort needed.

Understanding the reasons behind the customs can also be a means of counteracting ethnocentrism. In countries where very little protein is available, rats can be a good source of this important part of a healthy diet. Using cow dung mixed with mud to plaster houses made of mud and sticks seems to have a disinfectant effect. Where water is a precious commodity, daily baths just to remove odor would probably be considered an extravagant waste.

ACCEPTANCE: PRETENSE AND REALITY

Acceptance of the host people by the missionary is probably a difficult quality to define or measure. If asked, few missionaries would say, "I just could not accept the people I was living with" even though they may have left the field after only a few months. Surveys tend to show that the reasons given by missionaries for leaving the field are health, family problems, children's education, and burnout, but never lack of acceptance.[6]

What, then, constitutes acceptance? Dictionaries use a number of different terms to explain the concept: "To receive gladly," "to receive as adequate or satisfactory," "to be favorably disposed toward," "to regard as usual, proper, or right," "to believe in." All of these factors probably play an important part in becoming bicultural.

A number of years ago, a veteran missionary, when building a new mission house, built a special cement bench in the living room where the nationals were invited to sit. Although he had lived and worked on the mission field for over forty years, faced countless personal dangers with national pastors, lived with them in village huts, eating whatever they ate, he was never able to accept them as equal. They were not permitted to sit on the other furniture! Although this is an extreme illustration, it may well reflect the unspoken, sublimated attitude of missionaries who leave the field because of "family problems."

ADAPTATION AND/OR INTEGRATION

Myron Loss indicates that cross-cultural stress is increased in proportion to the person's involvement psychologically within the culture. It is more stressful to try to actively become a part of the host culture than to live in rather isolated American exclusivism. Although involvements, such as social relationships in ministry, business, recreation, and study, may at first be stressful, they are probably necessary for a missionary to reach his or her goals of cultural integration.[7]

Few missionaries would disagree with Loss. The difficulty comes in deciding how much integration is necessary for positive adaptation and effective ministry. E. Thomas Brewster and Elizabeth Brewster equate the bonding process of missionaries to a new culture to the bonding between infant and mother. This bonding needs to occur immediately after birth, when the infant is most sensitive and is psychologically and physiologically prepared to bond. This is necessary for a sense of belonging to be established. They contend that missionaries, immediately upon arrival on a new field, are best prepared for the bonding process. Because of the excitement engendered by the new environment, they are both psychologically and emotionally ready to become "belongers."

The Brewsters' suggestion, which has been adopted by several mission boards, is that new missionaries immediately become totally immersed in the new culture, living with a local family, dressing as they dress, eating the same food which has been prepared in the same way, and emulating completely their way of life, whether in a village or a city situation. In this way, the missionary becomes an insider, being more readily accepted by the people, and will have a more effective ministry.[8] Reed agrees with this method of bonding, which, he suggests, is also the best way of learning the new language. This identification with the people allows the missionary to become bicultural rather than monocultural, having learned to accept others as well as oneself.[9]

This method of bonding has been equated with the incarnational model established by Jesus. Just as Christ left heaven to become human to help humans establish a relationship with God, so the missionary needs to become a national to win nationals to this same relationship.[10]

Groups proposing this method of bonding cite Philippians 2:5–7, which discusses Christ's attitude about His incarnation. Kenneth McElhanon, in his defense of the incarnational method, quotes Paul Hiebert's model for missionary identification: (1) deep-level attitudes that cover ethnocentric feelings of cultural or racial superiority; (2) middle-level roles such as master-servant relationships; (3) surface-level cultural practices of lifestyle. If missionaries conform only to surface-level lifestyles, they will probably miss identification at deeper levels.

As McElhanon defines it, an incarnational ministry is an identification that goes much deeper than "the superficial material culture and behavior roles and focuses on the underlying attitudes that should characterize missionaries as servants."[11] If a missionary's lifestyle interferes with his or her ministry, then the lifestyle should be changed. Equating the incarnational model with mere physical or emotional deprivation is living on the surface-level of cultural practices. Such a model goes beyond merely giving up comfort and friends to an actual feeling of oneness with the host people.

The apostle Paul's method of becoming all things to all people (1 Cor. 9:19–23) is also cited as the incarnational method. However, Paul, whenever possible, went first to the synagogue and to his own ethnic race in every city he visited. He lived with his own kind until rejected by them. He ministered to the Jew first. He even lived with people who practiced his trade of tent-making (Acts 18:3). No amount of hardship or rejection made Paul abandon his ministry—which should be the same for the modern missionary, no matter what lifestyle he or she adopts.

Those advocating bonding by a total integration into the lifestyle of the host country are quick to point out that the purpose of bonding is a commitment to relationships at a deep level.[12] Several questions need to be asked about the bonding process. Does bonding necessarily lead to commitment? Is integration into a new lifestyle true bonding? Unless a missionary is from the same ethnic background as the people being ministered to, is it possible for him to be "incarnate" in that culture? Jesus was born a Jew, He grew up in a Jewish culture, He ate Jewish food from the time He was weaned, and He had Jewish brothers and sisters by blood as well as a Jewish mother. At what moment did He come to the understanding that He was divine as well as human, God as well as Jew? No matter what theological position is taken, it must be acknowledged that Christ was an ethnic Jew when He came to a knowledge of His divinity. He was a minister to His own ethnic group and not to Gentiles.

Recruiting people from ethnic backgrounds to minister as missionaries to their own ethnic group is another possibility for facilitating the integration process. Messianic Jews are returning to Israel to witness as missionaries (although they would not be known as such in the host country). Italian-Americans have for many years been recruited as missionaries to Italy, as have other ethnic Europeans, especially since the end of communism in Eastern Europe. Many times these recruits already have some knowledge of the language and customs because of their own backgrounds, lessening the stress of adaptation or bonding. The same has been true for Hispanic and Oriental recruits, for much of their original culture, including language, has been brought into their Western homeland. However, this has not been true for black, or African-Americans, returning as missionaries to

Africa; their original culture and language have been lost over the centuries. Several mission boards are actively trying to recruit black Americans as missionaries to Africa. Although they have the same problems of adjustment to the new culture as whites, the people in the host country seem to feel a greater affinity to them.[13]

Another factor that needs to be considered in the bonding process is that the baby is totally dependent on the mother, unable to live without her or a surrogate. To what extent is the missionary willing to become totally dependent on the host country? As Harriet Hill has aptly pointed out, Western Protestant missionaries do not become dependent on the host country even when they attempt to follow the incarnational model. They always have other funds at their disposal, which can be used as escape mechanisms. She claims that the model is not realistic since it cannot be followed to its logical end. The model is not honest, for the missionary does not intend to spend the rest of his or her life, without a break, living as a national in the host country. Neither is it necessarily appreciated by the host people since the missionary, knowing a better way of life, does not share this way.[14]

In the bonding process, the mother must also bond to the child, giving of herself, her time, energy, and desires, to fulfill the needs of her baby. Her bonding time continues far beyond the first few days, weeks, or months. For meaningful relationships to exist, a commitment has to be made by the insiders, the host people, as well as by the outsiders, the missionaries. Because of the attrition rate of new couples, veteran missionaries and national church leaders on one African field decided to have a joint prayer retreat at a remote mission station. Since all parties were fluent in the local language and deeply committed to a relationship that would help the church grow numerically and spiritually, communication was open and frank. The leadership of the national church wanted to know how they could modify their behavior to help new missionaries adjust! They accepted blame for the loss of the missionaries and wanted to know what they could do to change the situation. As a result of the discussions, a number of concrete suggestions were adopted as national church policy, such as forbidding pastors to solicit funds from missionaries. These suggestions greatly alleviated some of the frustrations of those trying to adapt to the culture.[15]

During this same meeting, the missionaries asked if they would be more effective in their ministry if they lived as the nationals. The reply was, "Why should you live like us if you don't have to? We are proud of you and glad that you can live as you do. You have shown us how to have better living standards and someday, as the Lord blesses our ministry, we want to live as you do." As living standards improve in third world countries, especially as more and more missionaries are living in large, modern cities, the differences in living styles no longer exist. Insiders and outsiders at times live in the same apartment complexes, shop in the same shops, eat in the same restaurants, and drive the same kinds of vehicles.

On the other hand, Jacob Loewen has noted several dangers associated with insider roles. Conflict occurs unless the missionary turns away completely from his or her own culture and people. Also, selecting only one or two insider roles does not cover enough of the lifestyle and the host people will expect the missionary's loyalty to them to exceed his or her loyalty to all other principles or people. "Missionary loyalty to principle rather than to his adopted people will automatically cause the alien insider to be labeled a traitor."[16]

Living a simpler lifestyle than what's considered normal in a Western culture, if necessary to become a more effective witness, would seem to be desirable. However, attention needs to be focused not on externals but on internals. Acceptance of the host people by the missionary is an intangible quality that cannot truly be expressed in words or actions but which will be understood through a mental attitude that permeates all relationships. Loewen considers outsider roles not only culturally safer but also probably more honest. "Full acceptance of the alien is not dependent on being inside, but on transparent honesty and reciprocity."[17]

Acceptance and commitment cannot be separated in the adjustment process. As the Brewsters mentioned, commitment to relationships is most important in the bonding process. However, as today's missionary often has to work with a strong, independent national church, commitment to the goals of that organization becomes more important than to individual relationships. In fact, in many countries, the national church selects the roles for the missionaries and may actually ask the mission organization to send only missionaries with qualifications for specific tasks. The missionary is no longer considered either an insider or an outsider but a partner in the biblical injunction to preach the gospel to all people and to build the church of Jesus Christ.[18]

As a partner, the missionary could then effectively perform the necessary outsider roles, mentioned by Loewen, as the provider of new information, as a source of reference, or as an agent who is able to establish contact with another group.[19] The latter is especially important in the distribution of foreign aid.

WITHDRAWAL

One of the alternatives to adaptation or integration is withdrawal, conscious or unconscious. The home or office becomes an isolation ward. Although missionaries continue to function in the workplace, psychologically and emotionally they have withdrawn from involvement with the host country and people. They perform their task capably but refuse to have any contact apart from that necessary to do their job. The following withdrawal techniques mentioned by Bernard and Huckins are probably being used by some missionaries as defense mechanisms to handle excess anxiety from seemingly impossible situations.

Repression is selectively putting out of mind any material that may be unacceptable, threatening, and anxiety-producing.[20] The missionary consciously chooses to ignore problems relating to the work, acting as though they do not exist; therefore they do not have to be dealt with. Because antipathy is an unacceptable response in relations with the host people, it will be denied and repressed rather than being acknowledged and overcome. As an example, on one field, the missionaries were in complete control of all church-related functions. When the young pastors wanted to organize with national leadership, the missionaries threatened to cut off all financial and food aid. They insisted that the pastors were too immature to make wise decisions when in actuality the missionaries were not ready to face potential conflicts with an independent church organization.

When a situation becomes self-demeaning or pressuring, *fantasy* substitutes imaginary and more pleasant thoughts for reality.[21] The missionary sees himself as adequately accomplishing the assigned task when in reality he may be causing discord on the field or in the national church. If he feels he must always look on the bright side, he may lose touch with the reality of the situation. This can easily happen when corruption is evident in church leadership. It is less anxiety producing to extol all the positive actions of the guilty party than to confront the problem.

Denial of reality, closely related to repression and fantasy, is the refusal to admit that discomforting material exists.

The person who uses denial as a means of reducing pressure and anxiety does so by developing reactions that make his participation impossible. (1) He may point out all kinds of reasons why a proposed course of action will not work. He promotes as many doubts as possible concerning the wisdom of moving toward a certain objective. (2) He may develop a headache or some other ailment that prevents his entering the stressful situation. (3) He may escape into reality by claiming that some other activity, like working at the office, is so demanding that he has neither time nor energy for the anxiety-provoking activity. (4) Or he may simply decide to act as though the happening that demands action from him has not taken place.[22]

One missionary became physically ill almost every time a field meeting was announced, and thus did not have to attend these pressure-filled conferences.

Negativism, a part of denial, often results when the missionary continues to find himself in a situation he can neither control nor change. Any action or project that he did not instigate or that did not receive his approval cannot possibly be "part of God's plan." He is quick to point out all the faults of the national pastors, the national church, other missionaries, and his living conditions.

Insulation is a way of protecting against hurt and disappointment by remaining aloof, uninvolved, and unapproachable. It is emotional blunting whereby the missionary continues to function without emotional involvement or commitment to the situation. Relationships are no longer considered important and emotions are repressed rather than controlled. Life may be lacking in excitement but it is also less challenging.

Isolation occurs when the individual cuts himself off completely from stress-producing situations. Attitudes are segregated which, if considered together, would produce conflict or anxiety. Isolation can occur when the person removes himself from the situation or activity either physically or emotionally, that is, by "disassociating one deeply rooted idea or conviction from another thoroughly ingrained, but antithetic, ethic or value."[23]

REJECTION

Stress and pressure are an integral part of adjustment to an alien culture. If adaptation and adjustment are not easily effected, tension results, which may be indicative of mixed feelings, ambivalence, and conflict.[24] When tension becomes excessive, total rejection occurs and the missionary resigns from the field.

Often missionaries do not look within themselves for the cause of their problems. Nor do they perceive themselves as being a part of the problem. To retain self-esteem, blame is generally placed on some outside source. If outside forces cannot be changed, rejection often occurs, resulting in resignation, although continued ministry would be possible with proper counseling, leading to a more accurate perception of their contribution to the problem.

Missionaries go to foreign fields to carry out the Great Commission given by Jesus in Matthew 28:19, "Go and make disciples of all nations, baptizing them in the name of the Father and of the Son and of the Holy Spirit." The process of fulfilling the commission may require a number of adjustments by the one called. For the message to be received, the missionary will probably have to establish an effective relationship with the host people. This relationship has been referred to as bonding, or establishing firm attachments to the host community. It has been suggested that for bonding to take place, there has to be genuine acceptance of the customs and culture of the host country. If the individual cannot make this adjustment, he or she may withdraw from involvement in the local society or completely from overseas service.

---

[1]Kalervo Oberg, "Cultural Shock: Adjustment to New Cultural Environments," *Practical Anthropology* 7 (1960): 177–82.

[2]Marjory F. Foyle, *Overcoming Missionary Stress* (Wheaton, Ill.: Evangelical Missions Information Service, 1987), 100.

[3]Harold W. Bernard and Wesley C. Huckins, *Dynamics of Personal Adjustment*, 2d ed. (Boston: Holbrook Press, 1975), 205; Lyman E. Reed,

Preparing Missionaries for Intercultural Communication: A Bicultural Approach (Pasadena, Calif.: William Carey Library, 1985), 21–22.

[4]Reed, *Preparing Missionaries*, 21–25, 143–44.

[5]Ibid., 88–89.

[6]Frank Allen, "Why Do They Leave? Reflections on Attrition," *Evangelical Missions Quarterly* 22 (April 1986): 118–28.

[7]Myron Loss, *Culture Shock: Dealing with Stress in Cross-Cultural Living* (Winona Lake, Ind.: Light and Life Press, 1983), 55.

[8]E. Thomas Brewster and Elizabeth S. Brewster, *Bonding and the Missionary Task* (Pasadena, Calif.: Lingua House, 1982), 1–10.

[9]Reed, *Preparing Missionaries*, 143–44.

[10]Brewster and Brewster, *Bonding*, 7.

[11]Kenneth McElhanon, "Don't Give Up on the Incarnational Model," *Evangelical Missions Quarterly* 27 (October 1991): 390–93.

[12]Brewster and Brewster, *Bonding*, 28.

[13]Rev. Keith Parks, director of missions, Southern Baptist Convention, Richmond, Va., and the area directors of the Assemblies of God Division of Foreign Missions, Springfield, Mo., interviewed by Marge Jones, 1991.

[14]Harriet Hill, "Incarnational Ministry: A Critical Examination," *Evangelical Missions Quarterly* 26 (August 1990): 196–201.

[15]Peggy Johnson and JoAnn Butrin, Assemblies of God missionaries to Isiro, Zaire, interviewed by Marge Jones, 1985.

[16]Jacob A. Loewen, "Roles Relating to an Alien Social Structure," *Missiology: An International Review* 4 (April 1976): 217–42.

[17]Ibid.

[18]Summary of Morris O. Williams, *Partnership in Mission: A Study of Theology and Method in Mission* (Springfield, Mo.: Empire Printing, 1979).

[19]Loewen, "Roles," 229–33.

[20]Bernard and Huckins, *Dynamics*, 234–35.

[21]Ibid., 235–36.

[22]Ibid., 236–37.

[23]Ibid., 237–38.

[24]Ibid., 197.

Chapter Five

The Letdown

Although the criteria for choosing missionary candidates could be as varied as the mission boards that hold them, several attributes would probably appear on all lists, such as strongly motivated, good self-concept, high achiever, and experienced. Some candidates may have felt a vocation since childhood, preparing for many years for a life-service overseas. In most, if not all, cases, the candidates will have had successful career experience in their home country or they would not have been accepted by the mission board.

Harold Bernard and Wesley Huckins found that a person projects the self he would like to become into an occupational situation, using the job as a means of becoming that self.[1] The candidate before going to the field has already projected himself into the work situation. Through the orientation process, he has studied the culture, the country, and the situation. He has probably talked with missionaries and nationals who have impressed on him the desperate need on the field and how he is uniquely qualified to meet the need.

Western society is strongly success oriented. All bookstores, both secular and religious, carry how-to books. As David Cummings noted, "The implication is that if we just follow this or that for-

65

mula, we will be successful."[2] Candidates have learned the formulas in their preparation process. They leave for the field with the latest spiritual and material tools necessary for the ministry. They have been God-called and God-endowed for their calling.

The new missionary is encumbered with a number of expectations:

1. Self-expectations
2. Perceived national church expectations
3. Mission board expectations
4. Supporting church expectations
5. Missionary colleagues' expectations

Many of these expectations may be unrealistic, for example, a desire for immediate fluency in the language, an immediate acceptance by and close relationship with nationals, and a satisfying, gratifying ministry with results during the first few years of service. Failure to reach these expectations could greatly affect a person's self-concept.

Bernard and Huckins state that "[p]robably *the focal* aspect of man's adjusting is his self-concept. One's self-concept influences the way he sees people, opportunities, obstacles, failures, and successes. . . . As one matures, his self-concept comes to be influenced by the skills, knowledge, and competencies he develops."[3] Candidates have developed the skills and gained the knowledge and competencies recommended for their ministry. With this strong self-concept, their expectations for success are generally high.

SHATTERED IDEALS

Why then are 20 percent to 50 percent[4] of new missionaries failing to return to the field after their first term? As has already been noted, adjusting to a new culture produces stress which can reduce achievement. If self-expectation slightly exceeds performance, this may lead to higher achievement. But for new missionaries, self-expectation could greatly exceed performance, creating even greater internal turmoil and conflict. When they discover that they cannot accomplish what they feel they should be accomplishing, their ideals can be shattered and discouragement and a sense of failure can result.

Janice Dixon has listed several major causes of frustrated expectations. One cause is naive expectations based on self-image. Because the sending churches think of missionaries as superpeople, new missionaries go to the field feeling that they are God's answer to any problem. They expect to see instant results, feeling that they have missed God's call if these do not materialize. They also go to the field eager to make friends, expecting the same eagerness from the host people. However, they often discover that, rather than being treated as welcome guests, they are regarded as unwelcome intruders. The sentiment may well be, "Yankee, go home, but keep on sending us your money!"

Other causes mentioned by Dixon are the problems of adjusting to a new culture, different living conditions, and family problems. Many times the wife, who is left out of the excitement of the work but carries a lot of the burden, finds adjustment impossible. "The new missionary, picked for leadership skills and all-around talent at home, suddenly is thrown into the role of a learner, a student begging for a chance to serve. No one knows his or her worth, or even cares. But rather than losing self-confidence, the new missionary may need to revise expectations and find a way to be accepted on local terms."[5]

Candidates may also have an unrealistic expectation of the spirituality of the national church leadership. When sending reports to their home churches, missionaries will naturally write spiritual success stories, dwelling on the strengths of their national colleagues rather than on their weaknesses. Arriving on the field, however, new missionaries are suddenly faced with frailties and failures among those whom they had considered spiritual giants. They may also find that the accepted standard for Christian living is much lower than the expected biblical standards in their home church or denomination. They are often faced with the dilemma of working closely with an organization with whom they do not agree on any number of principles.

Veteran missionaries can also be a part of the letdown process. The personable, dynamic speaker who seemed so warm and caring suddenly becomes a workaholic, expecting the new missionary to find his or her niche, learn the language, and do the work assigned. The expected time for spiritual refreshing together never materializes. Although the new missionary may well feel that the veteran's lifestyle and philosophy of missionary work are antiquated, they are the norm for the field.

Another source of frustration can be the mission board, whose attitude toward the appointed missionary may seem different from that perceived by the cultivated candidate. Helpful hints may well become ultimatums as the honeymoon turns into a serious working relationship in which the new missionary is accountable to the board for all his or her actions. Even in the few situations where an eight-hour workday exists, the missionary is on twenty-four-hour duty and can be called to task for anything he or she does during what might be called leisure time as well as during ministry time. John Doe has become John Missionary with the feeling that the individual has been swallowed up by the ministry.

FACING REALITY

Dixon and Cummings agree that one of the most important ingredients in facing reality is the time factor. Cummings maintains that success-oriented candidates, reflecting the society that has nurtured them, will expect quick results and will often have short-term commitments to a specific task. They will be critical of veteran missionaries who may have worked for five or ten years before seeing concrete results. "When their own programs don't produce results within the time frame allotted, they may fold their tents and go home."[6]

Dixon feels that new missionaries need to have a long-term view of who they are in God's plan and recognize the time and effort needed to develop fruitful work. God is molding servants who need to learn to take orders and to submit. "He desires Spirit-filled servants who develop fruit of the Spirit as well as gifts of the Spirit, to advance against the kingdom of darkness. . . . To survive, missionaries need prayer, a willingness to grow, and common-sense expectations."[7]

Another reality that new missionaries must face is that they now work with a group, that most of the world is made up of relational societies where people look out for each other rather than for self. Group decisions control all the actions of the individuals whether or not they agree with the policy. Cummings points out that Western society's emphasis on independence hinders its missionaries' ability to function in a relational way.[8]

Therefore, interdependence needs to be taught with the realization that a person cannot be committed to another person or group and still maintain his or her independence. That is, the individual's personal desires may have to be subject to the will of the group.

Fred Renich suggests the following as reasonable goals for first-term missionaries:

1. A good foundation in the language.
2. Satisfactory adjustment to the climate, customs, culture and people on his field.
3. A thorough working knowledge of the mission.
4. An understanding of the field, its problems, demands, and potential.
5. Some awareness of his gifts and place in the work.
6. A deepening confirmation of his call as a result of a growing sense of belonging and a consciousness of being useful.[9]

Cummings suggests that mission boards need to take more time to train, disciple, and channel those who are the products of our society's emphasis on independence, goal setting, and success, for these attitudes will be "counterproductive and destructive in the relational societies to which most of our candidates go." The goals set by the board or the individual may not be God's goals or geared to His timetable. Missionary Paul expected instant converts when he gave his testimony in Damascus after his conversion experience. Instead, he barely escaped with his life, and then spent three years in the desert, learning how to integrate his Old Testament knowledge with new covenant theology (Acts 9:20–25; Gal. 1:15–18). Bible scholars estimate that fifteen years passed between Paul's conversion and his first missionary journey.[10]

BOGGED DOWN IN DETAILS

One missionary who withdrew from the field during his first term wrote, "I found that the missionary 'success stories' are very rare exceptions to the overwhelming mass of routine or unsuccessful activities of the missionary's day."[11] Many of the activities necessary to living in third world countries have little or no relation to the missionary's perceived ministry. Buying food, getting fuel, paying bills, going from one government office to another for necessary visas, work permits, building permits, or any number of other permits necessary for daily activities will often take up the majority of the missionary's time. Prayer, Bible study, and preparation for work ministry are often relegated to the hours between 7 P.M. and 7 A.M., leaving little or no time for family life, recreation, and much-needed fellowship.

Another frustrating but very necessary part of missionary life is the paperwork required by the mission board. Because of increasing government regulations on nonprofit organizations, the need for detailed financial reports is mandatory. Many missionaries find themselves accountable for large sums of money designated for the national church, whether or not they have had accounting or bookkeeping. There may be routine progress reports to the mission board and/or sending churches. In those organizations where missionaries are responsible to raise their own funds, there is the need for constant contact with supporting churches or individuals.

Although all these routine activities have been explained during orientation, new candidates have little concept of how time-consuming such activities will become. Focus is, and should be, directed toward work ministry, building vision, excitement, and expectation. Some mission boards now recruit short-term personnel specialized in office procedures, especially accounting. Also, on a number of fields, qualified nationals are hired to handle routine duties, including those dealing with government agencies. Some mission boards send out full-time missionaries as business agents whose only duties are to take care of these onerous but necessary details.

<h2>ADMINISTRATIVE HEADACHES</h2>

To illustrate the stress of having to make decisions, E. Rae Harcum reported a famous experiment done by J. V. Brady. Brady placed pairs of monkeys in restraining chairs. Electric shocks were given to both at regular intervals. One monkey, designated the "executive," could turn off the shock for both itself and the other monkey by pushing a lever. However, the executive monkey usually developed stomach ulcers; the other did not, even though both received the same number of shocks.[12]

Administration, because of the very nature of overseas work, becomes, to some degree, a part of every missionary's life. As the representative of a foreign agency, whether in some remote village or a teeming metroplex, whether working alone or with dozens of compatriots, each missionary will have administrative duties. A number of mission boards have all the missionaries on any given field organized in some sort of fellowship with a chairperson or moderator, secretary, and treasurer. Committees are formed for evangelism, education, medical work, and many other projects.

On fields having limited missionary personnel, new missionaries may well find themselves with administrative duties they are not prepared for and do not feel capable of accomplishing. But because they want to cooperate, to fit in with the team, or simply to do a job that must be done because there is no one else to do it, they find themselves with unwanted responsibilities. Marjory Foyle gives three fundamentals for administrative appointments. The pattern for appointing and changing administrative personnel should be written into the constitution. Persons gifted for the job and with the proper qualifications should be trained and appointed. An impartial third party should be available to hear legitimate complaints against the administration.[13]

Myron Loss has suggested fifteen tips for survival, which may help alleviate much of the letdown experienced by first-term missionaries:

1. Set reasonable goals.
2. Don't take your job description too seriously.
3. Be committed to joy.
4. Maintain good emotional health.
5. Remember that you are human.
6. Don't be afraid of being a little bit eccentric.
7. Be flexible.
8. Don't take yourself too seriously.
9. Reduce your stress where possible.
10. Make your cultural change gradual.
11. Forgive yourself; forgive others.
12. Establish some close friendships with people from the host culture.
13. Be thankful.
14. Be an encourager.
15. Take courage; someone understands.[14]

Perhaps what Loss is suggesting is that the letdown process will be greatly diminished as new missionaries learn to remove

CHAPTER

5

**The
Letdown**

their mask of perfection. Recognizing their own limitations, admitting to their own problems and shortcomings, asking for help when needed, not expecting too much of themselves or others, will help them face reality without losing sight of their goals.

[1] Harold W. Bernard and Wesley C. Huckins, *Dynamics of Personal Adjustment* (Boston: Holbrook Press, 1975), 302.

[2] David Cummings, "Programmed for Failure—Mission Candidates at Risk," *Evangelical Missions Quarterly* 23 (July 1987): 240–46.

[3] Bernard and Huckins, *Dynamics*, 22–23.

[4] Because statistics change each year with each mission board, exact percentages are difficult to obtain.

[5] Janice Dixon, "Unrealistic Expectations: The Downfall of Many Missionaries," *Evangelical Missions Quarterly* 26 (October 1990): 388–93.

[6] Cummings, "Programmed for Failure," 240–46.

[7] Dixon, "Unrealistic Expectations," 388–93.

[8] Cummings, "Programmed for Failure," 240–46.

[9] Fred C. Renich, "First-Term Objectives," *Evangelical Missions Quarterly* 3 (Summer 1967): 209–17.

[10] Cummings, "Programmed for Failure," 240–46.

[11] Cary Tidwell, secretary of Personnel and Family Life Department, Assemblies of God Division of Foreign Missions, Springfield, Mo., interviewed by Marge Jones, July 1992.

[12] E. Rae Harcum, *Psychology for Daily Living: Simple Guidance in Human Relations for Parents, Teachers, and Others* (Chicago: Nelson-Hall, 1979), 119–20.

[13] Marjory F. Foyle, *Overcoming Missionary Stress* (Wheaton, Ill.: Evangelical Missions Information Service, 1987), 118.

[14] Myron Loss, *Culture Shock: Dealing with Stress in Cross-Cultural Living* (Winona Lake, Ind.: Light and Life Press, 1983), 85–101.

Chapter Six

The Goldfish Bowl

"It is so quiet here!" José, a theology student from Puerto Rico, was talking with a fellow student shortly after arriving in the United States. "In my country we have noise pollution so if you want quiet you have to use ear plugs." He went on to say that stores advertised with loud speakers, each one competing with the next. Radios and televisions were turned up loud enough for all neighbors to hear, day and night. If parties were held, often until two o'clock in the morning, the music could generally be heard for blocks. Even if the police were called, they wouldn't respond. "You want to sleep," he said in his broken English, "you put in ear plugs!"[1]

Noise pollution is a way of life in many urban areas of the third world. But the underlying idea is not the proliferation of noise as such but the thought that whatever each individual has should be shared with others. If my neighbor does not have a radio, then mine should be played with enough volume for him to enjoy it. My TV should be placed in such a way that he can watch it through a window. My party should be loud enough for him to participate though not actually present in the building.

"We share everything with our neighbors," José continued. "My neighbor used to bring over food for us every day. If anyone came to our house saying that they had no food or money, we would give it to them." Medications, which were sometimes hard to come by, were usually passed around as needed. Neighbors were also expected to interfere in each other's problems. He cited several examples of family problems, especially those that involved physical abuse, where neighbors stepped in to help.

An individual's right to privacy often has a different connotation overseas. "My personal problems are private if they involve only me but if the problem is social, then it is not private," José continued. When asked if he found Western missionaries to be distant, the response was an emphatic no. "Missionaries have come to my country because they like my country and culture. I don't treat them in a special way." But, coming to the States, José found a different situation. He was surprised to find Christians standoffish and very closed. "They don't greet me when I pass and don't pick me up when I am waiting for a bus, even if they are going in my direction. In Puerto Rico, we would pick up somebody we knew and take him where he needed to go, even if we were going somewhere else."

Before leaving for the field, most candidates owned their own vehicle. This vehicle was their private property to be used as they wished when they wished. However, overseas they will probably be using transportation that belongs to the mission. These vehicles and who has the right to use them has long caused problems. José felt very strongly about the insensitivity and selfishness of individuals who had room in their cars but wouldn't offer a ride to a friend. To many Westerners, even when used for business purposes, for commuting, or for carpooling, the family car belongs, in a very personal way, to the family. Drives in the country to "get away from it all" often become longed for and necessary times of privacy and solitude. Commercials for new cars invariably show individuals, couples, or families driving through isolated stretches of wilderness or headed to sparsely populated beaches.

This ingrained concept of the privacy of one's means of transport cannot quickly be eliminated from a new missionary's way of thinking. Some mission boards supply mission vehicles for church use and allow individual missionaries to purchase separate, private vehicles for personal use.[2] The problem arises whether the missionary is traveling to a church-related function or going on vacation. If the trip is to a church conference, just who and how many should ride with the missionary leads to much discussion. One veteran missionary tells the local church leader exactly how many people and how much baggage he is willing to take and the decision is then left with the national leadership. (He also has established a firm, nonnegotiable policy that he will transport *no* dried fish in his vehicle!)

If the individual missionary is going on a personal trip, perhaps on vacation or to visit children at a boarding school, the situation becomes more complicated. Often a couple has looked forward to this time alone, considering the time they are traveling to be just as much a part of their vacation as the time in the game parks or visiting national monuments. But, in situations where public transport is practically nonexistent, nationals feel that any partially empty car traveling in their direction should be available to them. This is part of "Christian" ethics. To avoid this problem, one missionary couple traded their mission station wagon for a Volkswagen bug and had suitcases especially made, one each for mother, father, and the two boys, to fit in the front trunk. Resentment about this attitude, as well as the psychological source it originated from, caused the missionary to be transferred from the field and, eventually, from overseas service.

The right to privacy has become more of a legal problem than a psychological one in most Western countries. The rights of government to use electronic eavesdropping equipment has been, and will continue to be, debated through the court system. This is not a problem in third world countries, seldom interested in bugging missionary homes, even if they had the equipment to do so. But a type of bugging, which is not electronic, does exist and, although seldom mentioned, can be devastating to new missionaries. José would call this a normal Christian interest in your neighbor's affairs. Christian nationals tend to feel that every aspect of "their" missionary's life belongs to them.

The idea that a man's home is his castle was succinctly expressed by the eighteenth-century English statesman William Pitt: "The poorest man may, in his cottage, bid defiance to all the forces of the Crown. It may be frail; its roof may shake; the wind may blow through it; the storm may enter; the rain may enter; but the King of England may not enter; all his force dares not cross the threshold of the ruined tenement."[3] Missionaries may, at times, have their homes entered by government agencies, especially where government coups occur on a monthly or yearly basis. Such crises, although traumatic due to the Western principle that "a man's home is his castle," cannot be avoided and are generally accepted as part of modern missionary ministry.

However, the psychological invasion of missionary homes by nationals is much more subtle and intangible. To begin with, many missionary families have nationals in their homes to help with house or office work. Their understanding of English is often underestimated! But it is not necessary to understand the language to know when a husband and wife are having an argument, or when the children are misbehaving, or how much time the couple spends in Bible study and prayer. This information is often disseminated, not as gossip, but as a vital part of the nationals' interest in every facet of "their" missionary's life.

Nationals often have a sense of propriety over the missionary working with them. Even thirty years after the end of colonialism, domestic servants have a high standing in the community, whether village, town, or city. The accomplishments of the missionary become their accomplishments and his or her problems their problems. This is also generally true of the feelings of the church community. This invasion of a missionary's private life would not be considered prying but involvement in a valuable asset.

TRANSPARENCY

M. C. Slough started his book *Privacy, Freedom and Responsibility* with the following statement. "Practically everyone in these times has come to expect, if not demand, some measure of privacy. This necessarily involves the right to live at least part of one's life divorced from public interest and the public eye. It means living according to one's own individual choice and free from the probings of other people."[4]

The missionary has chosen to live according to the expectations of the church in his or her host country. Because of this, his or her life is no longer divorced from public interest and the public eye and, often, not from the probings of other people. It has been reported that "privacy is a prerogative that politicians no longer enjoy" after the scandal-ridden U.S. politics of the

1980s and early 1990s.[5] Perhaps missionaries should be included in this category.

Goldfish bowls are made to see through. Its inhabitants are not intimidated if they are watched while eating, swimming, fighting, or defecating. Is it possible for missionaries to live such transparent lives? There is a greater chance of some measure of anonymity in a large city, where missionaries can be more isolated although living in large apartment complexes. Old-style mission compounds continue to serve as very transparent goldfish bowls and certainly candidates going to villages or small towns need to be prepared for the intensive scrutiny they will be receiving.

J. Grant Howard, in talking about the necessity of transparency for open communication, concludes that transparency is very traumatic. "Open communication is like getting an immunization shot. It hurts, but it helps." He mentions that the need for, and the enjoyment of, isolation is one of the sociological factors that hinder communication. "So we build fences, mountain cabins, buy boats and campers, take trips—anything to get away from it all. Isolation doesn't always foster communication."[6] There is no immunization shot that can be given to new candidates against their need for privacy, but recognizing this need and facing the reality of goldfish-bowl living in most third world countries can help mission boards in the screening and preparation of those called to this ministry.

Vulnerability

At the same time, psychologist Sydney Jourard, in an article in *Law and Contemporary Problems*, wrote that "[t]he experience of psychotherapists and students of personality growth has shown that people maintain themselves in physical health and in psychological and spiritual well-being when they have a 'private place,' some locus that is inviolable by others except at the person's express invitation."[7] Stephen Goode, in talking about the right to privacy, mentions that privacy is important for several reasons. Each individual needs to have a sense of autonomy, feeling that an area of his or her life is totally under his or her own control, free from outside intrusion. "Without the right to privacy, there can be little human dignity or individuality."[8]

David and Vera Mace conducted a survey of pastors and their

wives, the results of which were reported in *Pastoral Psychology*. They found that lack of family privacy was cited as a problem by 52 percent of the husbands but only 32 percent of the wives. However, 68 percent of the wives felt deprived of time alone with their husbands because of lack of privacy.[9] Although pastors and their families in the States are under scrutiny, they do have methods of escape. They can get away to other towns for a few days or weeks, places where they are not known. More and more parishioners are being made aware that the pastor needs time alone with his or her family. Many, if not most, pastors no longer live next to the church.

The possibility of escape to some private place is probably even more important for missionary families because of being constantly surrounded by the people of the host country. If the children are sent away to boarding school, parents often find a time of legitimate escape when they leave the mission station to visit them. Some mission agencies even have permanent guest houses available near boarding schools especially for such occasions.

Nonmission friends can also provide havens away from the public eye. One missionary husband and wife, who lived very visible lives at a Bible school, were able to spend Christmas vacation at an embassy couple's comfortable apartment while they were away from the embassy, visiting the States. The missionaries returned to their work refreshed and renewed after their ten days of relative invisibility.

Orientation programs for mission candidates should have special counseling to prepare them for the goldfish bowl. Admittedly, candidates vary greatly in their extroversion, which is generally a plus in adapting to "visibility living." A highly introverted, private candidate who needs a great deal of solitude and privacy to function effectively should probably be assigned to a place where it's available. The missionary who bought the Volkswagen bug was, to all appearances, an excellent communicator. He was fluent in the local language, had an effective ministry at the Bible school, even writing a number of courses, had helped start several new churches, and seemed to be the ideal missionary. But everything he had done for the national church finally held very little significance for the national Christians, partially because of his attitude toward their invasion of his privacy.

[1]José Estrella, Central Bible College student, Springfield, Mo., interviewed by Marge Jones, August 1993. Used with permission.

[2]Several Baptist boards follow this policy.

[3]Stephen Goode, *The Right to Privacy* (New York: Franklin Watts, 1983), 55.

[4]M. C. Slough, *Privacy, Freedom and Responsibility* (Springfield, Ill.: Charles C. Thomas, 1969), 3.

[5]"Politicians and Privacy," *CQ Researcher*, 17 April 1992, 338.

[6]J. Grant Howard, *The Trauma of Transparency: A Biblical Approach to Interpersonal Communication* (Portland, Oreg.: Multnomah Press, 1979), 219, 165.

[7]Sydney Jourard, "Some Psychological Aspects of Privacy," *Law and Contemporary Problems* (Spring 1966).

[8]Goode, *Privacy*, 8.

[9]David R. Mace and Vera C. Mace, "Marriage Enrichment for Clergy Couples," *Pastoral Psychology* 30 (Spring 1982): 151–59.

Chapter Seven

Square Pegs and Round Holes

When the apostle Paul wrote to the Philippian Christians that he could do all things through Christ, who would give him strength (Phil. 4:13), he could not have foreseen the misery these words, when taken out of context, would cause thousands of missionaries following in his footsteps. If he had only written a commentary on these words—drawing attention to the fact that "all things" refers to what God wants one to do whether or not one has plenty of food and money—perhaps the mistakes made by those adhering to this letter could have been avoided. Viewing missionaries as superhuman beings who can accomplish any task assigned, whether qualified or not, because of this biblical promise has probably led to the resignation of many capable individuals who could have had a long and fulfilling ministry—in the right position.

Levi Keidel, when asking that missionaries not be treated like God, notes a number of outcomes from viewing missionaries unrealistically:

1. Missionaries try to perpetrate the false image that churches have projected on them.

2. Physical and mental brokenness, even occasionally self-destruction, result from the strain of trying to live beyond themselves.

3. Missionaries may attempt to manipulate those they minister to in an attempt to live up to and justify expectations.
4. The supporting churches and individuals, the very people missionaries need to minister to them, become alienated from the missionaries because they see the missionaries as above themselves, not experiencing the same struggles they identify as their own.[1]

In referring to recruitment pitfalls, Kenneth Gangel mentions three biases. One is the *availability bias*, which leads mission boards to grab the first candidate available when a need presents itself.

It may be admirable for a missionary trained in church planting to take over the deanship of the Bible institute, but his pliability and willingness do not substitute for training and expertise in the area into which we have thrust him. Just because a person is "there" does not mean he or she represents God's choice for that particular position.

The second bias is the *association bias*, leaders (missionaries) being chosen for one position because they were successful in another position. "Such an error forgets that leadership is always situational." Three important ingredients in any situation are the leader, the people he or she serves, and the situation he or she serves in. All three of these need to be considered when choosing a person for any position.

The third bias is the *agreement bias*, leaders being chosen who hold carefully to the "party line and have no record of rocking the boat. Never mind that they have no record of initiative, no vision, and no demonstration of capability toward supervising the work of others."[2] It is generally easier to choose a yes-man than a person who questions policies in order to improve them.

Few candidates would be chosen by any mission board who did not agree with the policies of that organization. Missionaries, of necessity, have to work as team members, adhering to the rules and regulations of the sending body as well as of the national organization. Few places are left where an individual can go into virgin territory and pioneer a work without having to answer to or work with someone. Although we want to get away from the "little kingdom concept," mission boards should allow missionaries to be individuals, using their individual

CHAPTER 7

Square Pegs and Round Holes

strengths and abilities in situations where these can best be applied. There is a difference between adhering to policy and becoming a "yes" person, where original ideas are stifled simply because they may seem contrary to those of the "boss."

One couple who had problems with language learning was sent to a field where two languages were required. Besides one other newly arrived couple, the only missionaries on the field were several single women who were firmly in control of most ministries. Instead of having an opportunity to use his pastoral experience, the husband was asked to spend all his time learning the second language. A strong disagreement arose over national church administration policies. These multiple pressures triggered a physical problem for the husband, causing the family to leave the field fifteen months later. Since arriving back in the United States, he has successfully pastored two churches, but his heart's cry is to return to the mission field. Had he been assigned to a field where a second language was not required and placed in a position where his pastor's heart and warm, outgoing nature could have been used, he may well have continued his overseas ministry for many years.

Self-Esteem

In the above example, the husband's self-esteem, or perceived self-worth, had probably been damaged when he had difficulty, even during nine months of study, learning French, the official language of the country he was going to. When he arrived on the field, he was immediately expected to study a rather difficult local language. His language aptitude test as well as his age (upper thirties) indicated that he would probably have difficulty learning even a simple language. Yet he was placed in a position of having to learn two difficult ones.

He probably became more frustrated, since he was not able to do the one thing he had been successful in—pastoring. His desire to meet people and minister to their spiritual needs was thwarted. The particular work he had been assigned was firmly under the control of one of the women who felt threatened by his arrival. Add to the above his physical condition, which required constant, strong medication, and the volatile situation that resulted could probably end only in disaster. It became impossible to reshape this square peg to fit a very round hole.

One evangelical missions organization requires the Tennessee Self-concept Scale, on which their missions candidates must score in the seventy-fifth to ninety-fifth percentile compared to the population norm. This indicates that they are far above the average in self-acceptance. Yet the same organization found that the biggest emotional problem of missionaries is that of low self-image. Somehow the positive self-image is being destroyed after they become missionaries.

When Christ told His followers to love their neighbors as they love themselves (Matt. 19:19), He was indicating that each person has self-worth. This self-love is not pride but, as Myron Loss has indicated, a love for one's own soul, an appreciation for the fact that each person is made in the image of God. He suggests that self-esteem is

the evaluation which an individual makes and customarily maintains with regard to himself. It expresses an attitude of approval or disapproval, and indicates the extent to which the individual believes himself to be capable, significant, successful and worthy.[3]

Feelings of security and significance are probably vital for self-esteem.

Ego expansion, or the desire to build self-esteem, and motivation go hand in hand. E. Rae Harcum states that a person will perform acts to protect his self-esteem and to enhance his conception of himself. He should also not be forced into taking a position from which retreat would cause him to look like a failure. Each situation should, if possible, be arranged to prevent the individual from making the incorrect response initially. As people assess themselves through the reactions of others, they need to feel valued and approved.[4] If the husband in the above illustration had been permitted to start a youth center immediately, the ministry that was on his heart, he would have had the contact with the young people that he needed and valued. He would have had a chance to use and improve his French with these educated teenagers rather than feeling a failure while trying to learn yet another language.

A stable person who is well adjusted, enjoying life, and achieving self-actualization is generally considered mentally healthy.[5] Harold Bernard and Wesley Huckins refer to these people as being "heterostatic," sufficiently self-confident to make decisions, accepting new experiences as a challenge and finding self-expression in any given activity. Risks in an uncertain future are considered tests of their strength and skill. Their desire to grow outweighs their defensive motives. "Homeostatic" people, on the other hand, generally avoid new experiences and self-initiated growth. They doubt their ability to learn new processes and find making decisions difficult.[6]

Experiencing and coping with challenging experiences generates self-confidence in both heterostatic and homeostatic individuals. The difference lies in the type of experiences that challenge them. If the individual considers himself or herself capable of meeting the challenge and accomplishing the assigned task, self-confidence will grow. Mission boards need to realize that, although Paul became all things to all men (1 Cor. 9:22), few missionaries are capable of continual transformational shifts.

One missionary who had homeostatic tendencies worked for a number of years on a remote mission station, where he could control his activities and contacts with the national church. He was faithful in ministering in the local churches, encouraging pastors and holding Bible teaching sessions (with the help of his wife) for those who wanted to go into the ministry. Few new churches were started and the local congregations grew very slowly, if at all. Because there seemed to be no progress in the national work, the family was moved to another city in another country, where the couple was given office-type work under the direct supervision of a heterostatic individual. The situation deteriorated rapidly with some harsh accusations being made by all parties. After twenty years of missionary service, this couple was asked to resign and forced to leave the country and the people they had grown to love. Feeling like total failures, their self-esteem was decimated because they were put into a situation they could not cope with.

Rather than trying to find alternative solutions to personality, situational, or emotional problems, mission boards often seem to look for a spiritual solution. When stressful situations arise, they would agree with Marjory Foyle, who suggests three steps in adapting to stress. First, the missionary needs to realize that he or she is not alone, for God has promised His presence. Second, missionaries need to use all their own human courage to deal with the situation. Third, missionaries need to use their anger creatively by controlling it and directing it in a situation where change for the better can be effected.[7] The power of the Holy Spirit to help in any situation should never be minimized, but hurting, frustrated individuals in seemingly impossible circumstances may have difficulty in understanding just what the Holy Spirit is saying.

WASTED POTENTIAL

Asking missionaries to continue working in situations where they do not feel comfortable or capable of accomplishing the task may often be wasting their potential for another area. One couple who felt called to a large city in a certain country was sent to a remote mission station in another country—"because of the great need." The missionary, who had no mechanical abilities whatsoever, then had to cope with a power plant, water pump, deteriorating house, kerosene refrigerator, and an assortment of other technical jobs associated with daily living. Naturally, the couple found themselves, for one reason or another, driving into the capital, where they spent the best part of their term. Fortunately, they were then allowed to go to the country of their calling where they lived in a city and had a very fruitful ministry.

People reach self-actualization when they feel that they have become the most they are capable of becoming.[8] However, self-actualization is seldom considered necessary for missionary work. In fact, many missionaries would consider *selflessness* a very important part of their spiritual preparation for the ministry. This very desire to deny themselves may lead them into accepting positions that can cause acute stress.

Perhaps there has been a confusion between denial of human desires and the denial of human capability or incapability. The very fact that a person is willing to leave home, family, and friends to go into an unknown country, learn the language, adjust to different living conditions, and often minister under difficult situations indicates self-denial. However, for the person to effectively function anywhere, self-esteem, self-confidence, and some sense of control of the situation are necessary for emotional well-being as well as for effective job performance.[9]

Most mission boards would agree with Bernard and Huckins that today's missionaries need to achieve flexibility, self-initiative, and a tolerance for ambiguity in a rapidly changing world. In fact, one of humanity's most outstanding characteristics is its adaptability. Focus on the development of a robust self-concept with a desire for continuous learning will greatly help in the process of adjustment to any situation. Bernard and Huckins further state that actualized people can be either dependent or independent, according to the situation. They do not have to prove their ability to relate or to verify that they are acceptable. They have come to terms with all four major aspects of adjustment: physical, mental, emotional, and spiritual. In addition, they feel that the focus of control resides in themselves rather than outside forces, no matter what situation they are facing.[10]

The variety of opportunities for ministry in third world countries today is almost unlimited. With strong emerging indigenous national churches, the missionary is no longer limited to church planting and nurturing. There is a need for professional as well as ecclesiastical personnel. In many countries, builders, teachers, doctors, printers, accountants, counselors, engineers, and secretaries are needed just as much as pastors. In some situations the missionary still needs to be a jack-of-all-trades, but there is no longer a need to force all missionaries into this mold.

Furthermore, in many third world countries, visas are no longer granted to missionaries as such. To enter, a person must have some trade or profession that the country feels is needed. Restrictions are then sometimes placed on any type of religious activity. A number of young people are now ministering overseas as "tentmakers," earning their living by working at a profession in the host country while at the same time having a spiritual ministry.

However, as Foyle has pointed out, stress can be caused by the perceived difference between secular and spiritual work. Individuals may feel so overloaded with their secular work that they have no time left for so-called spiritual activity. A constant struggle results among the demands of home, work, and church. Sometimes the individual feels that only church-related work is ministry, rather than accepting both professional and spiritual activities as proclaiming the gospel of Christ.[11] Christ admonished His followers to be the salt of the earth whatever their status or position, bringing flavor to whoever was around them (Matt. 5:13).

Another reality that new missionaries have to face is that they cannot control the demands made upon them by the host people. For example, mission doctors who have specialized in pediatrics or gynecology will be expected to perform all necessary surgery. In a remote village clinic, the mission doctor will be expected to operate on a strangulated hernia to save a life whether having performed such a procedure before. Secular teachers will be expected to conduct Bible classes whether they have had formal biblical training. In some countries, cultural conflicts will be caused by saying no to such requests. So some way has to be found to get around the situation without having to refuse.

A new missionary doctor and his wife were preparing to go to a fairly well-equipped mission hospital in a remote part of Africa. Besides his work in the hospital, the doctor would also be responsible for regular visits to village clinics. As a pediatrician, he planned to work mostly with children. When the local missionaries pointed out that he would be expected to perform surgery in life-threatening situations, he decided that he would need more training to adequately accomplish his task.

ESCAPE

When a missionary does find a situation intolerable, there are a number of ways of coping. One way would be to try to manipulate the factors causing the stress. In its broadest sense, according to Bernard and Huckins, all behavior can be said to be manipulative, for it has an effect on the behavior of others.[12] Changing opinions and modifying behavior to suit changing situations is a normal daily occurrence. However, when square pegs find it impossible to change their shape to fit the round hole, they may try to manipulate individuals or circumstances to reshape the hole.

Unfortunately, studies have shown that periods of stress and anxiety decrease an individual's ability to think creatively. It may be very difficult for the missionary to think of positive ways to change either his or her own actions or the actions of others to find a better fit. Manipulation also suggests a degree of control that missionaries may not have. A number of years ago the author conducted a survey on missionary job satisfaction. The only complaint missionaries mentioned was having no input in the decisions coming from headquarters. A missionary's access

CHAPTER 7

———

Square Pegs and Round Holes

to a person who has the authority to manipulate circumstances and situations could well help alleviate some problems of adjustment.[13]

Flight from the situation is an option that is often difficult for missionaries to accept because they feel that they have not fulfilled their call. They have failed the Lord; with His help they should have been able to accomplish any task given them. However, Foyle suggests that flight can be very healthy when the individual has chosen it deliberately.[14] This decision may be made immediately or after a period of trying to cope and adjust to the stressful environment. The person comes to a steady conviction that it would be wrong to remain where he or she is. In other words, the decision should not be reached impulsively or when the person is under emotional pressure.

Unhealthy flight is escape into illness, which occurs when stress continues so long that adaptation breaks down. Some symptoms are unusual irritability, excessive anxiety, loss of appetite, sleeplessness, and feelings of hopelessness.[15] Unhealthy flight also occurs when the missionary refuses to see self in the problem. Most mission boards have made surveys of the reasons missionaries leave their field. In very few cases did the missionary state that "the problem lies with me."[16] Perhaps then the availability of a qualified counselor could be a way of avoiding unhealthy flight, helping the missionary see himself or herself as well as the situation from an objective, nonthreatening point of view.[17]

Another healthy way of temporary escape is in vacation and leisure time. Although all mission boards encourage their missionaries to take time off from work each year, to get away from it all, lack of finances or other considerations may prevent them from having a complete change of scene. Good vacation spots may be nonexistent or too expensive in the host country. Many mission boards now allow their missionaries to return to their home country for vacations at least once during their term, generally at the missionary's expense.

Daily or even weekly leisure time is generally harder to program into a work schedule that often starts at 6 A.M. and doesn't end until well after 6 P.M. Recreation to the host people in many developing countries consists of visiting friends and relatives. There is no such thing as a day off. They may have a hard time understanding why a missionary, who has spent all day dealing with people, would not want to spend the evening talking with the pastor! Missionaries may appear to be distant and withdrawn if they spend their evenings playing tennis in a club that most nationals cannot afford to attend or playing Scrabble with other missionaries. An open and frank discussion with national church leadership can usually help them understand the missionary's emotional and physical need for a time-out. Jesus took time to be alone (Mark 1:35) even though the disciples did not always understand His need.

When missionaries choose not to escape from a seemingly impossible situation, they may find themselves using any one of the capitulatory modes of adjustment suggested by Bernard and Huckins:

1. *Introjection or internalization*—the individual adopts the value system of the host country as his or her own, absorbing the ethical and moral proscriptions of the society.
2. *Identification*—such as taking as one's own some of the attributes of the people and institutions one is associated with; a feeling of sharing in the achievements, status, and possessions of other persons.
3. *Rationalization*—foolish, irresponsible, and illogical behaviors are justified by finding socially acceptable reasons for such actions, which soften the impact of failure or disappointment.
4. *Projection*—such as placing the blame for one's own failures on others or to impute to someone else one's own unacceptable feelings, desires, and thoughts.
5. *Displacement*—a shift of emotional expression, usually anger and hostility, from the causal source to some other person or object.
6. *Sublimation*—which may be the substitution of a socially approved goal for one whose normal expression is not possible; substitution of safer, more acceptable activities for those which are expected.
7. *Compensation*—overreaction to make up for a real or imagined inadequacy. "Excellence in another activity may be sought as an indirect approach in order to cover a deficiency. . . . Gratification in one area may be sought as a substitute for a frustration or lack of satisfaction in another."[18]

Some introjection and identification are very much a part of positive adaptation for all missionaries, but total acceptance and use of nonbiblical codes of conduct would not be considered an appropriate means of reaching people with the gospel of Christ no matter the level of frustration. Even contextualization of the teachings of Christ could not condone the use of corruption in the spread of His message, although corruption may be a common way of life in the host country.

Although Gangel's emphasis is on leadership training, many of the principles he mentions could well help mission organizations foster feelings of self-esteem and self-actualization in their missionaries. He states that mission leaders need to develop

1. a climate of respect focusing on individual worth and dignity and encouraging people to contribute their ideas;
2. a climate of trust in which people learn to trust their own abilities and those of others, unthreatened by constant changes in policy and program;
3. a climate of acceptance where, within the appropriate boundaries, people have room to think and move, to consider changes in their own belief systems, and more important, in methods of ministry;
4. a climate of discovery which recognizes that new leaders will make mistakes, that alternative solutions need to be explored without the pressures of immediate answers, and with tolerance for ambiguity in the tough problems; and
5. a climate of depth—depth of spiritual dimensions in individual and corporate leaders and also depth "on the bench."[19]

---

[1]Summary of Levi Keidel, *Stop Treating Me Like God* (Carol Stream, Ill.: Creation House, 1971).

[2]Kenneth O. Gangel, "Developing New Leaders for the Global Task," *Evangelical Missions Quarterly* 25 (April 1989): 166–71.

[3]Myron Loss, *Culture Shock: Dealing with Stress in Cross-Cultural Living* (Winona Lake, Ind.: Light and Life Press, 1983), 26.

[4]E. Rae Harcum, *Psychology for Daily Living: Simple Guidance in Human Relations for Parents, Teachers, and Others* (Chicago: Nelson-Hall, 1979), 102, 83.

[5]Ibid., 129.

[6]Harold W. Bernard and Wesley C. Huckins, *Dynamics of Personal Adjustment,* 2d ed. (Boston: Holbrook Press, 1975), 45.

[7]Marjory F. Foyle, *Overcoming Missionary Stress* (Wheaton, Ill.: Evangelical Missions Information Service, 1987), 16–20.

[8]Spencer A. Rathus, *Psychology,* 2d ed. (New York: Holt, Rinehart and Winston, 1984), 257.

[9]Bernard and Huckins, *Dynamics*, 88.

[10]Ibid., 292, 417–26.

[11]Foyle, *Overcoming*, 115.

[12]Bernard and Huckins, *Dynamics*, 180.

[13]Marge Jones, "First-Year Counseling: A Key Ingredient to Success," *Evangelical Missions Quarterly* 29 (July 1993): 294–98.

[14]Foyle, *Overcoming*, 20.

[15]Ibid., 21.

[16]Survey conducted by the *Evangelical Missions Quarterly* 22 (April 1986): 123–29.

[17]Jones, "First-Year Counseling," 294–98.

[18]Bernard and Huckins, *Dynamics*, 240–49.

[19]Gangel, "Developing New Leaders," 166–71.

CHAPTER 7

Square Pegs and Round Holes

Chapter Eight

Dealing With Guilt

There was plenty of work to be done to prepare a meal for Jesus and His disciples (Luke 10:38–42). Martha, being a good hostess, accepted the fact that the visiting would have to wait until the meal was finished. Well-brought-up Jewish women knew cooking a good meal for guests not only was the proper conduct but also would bring praise for a job well done. Her sister, Mary, was certainly not doing her duty by sitting in the living room talking with Jesus. It simply was not fair! Martha enjoyed visiting with the Master, too, but first things had to come first. "'Lord, don't you care that my sister has left me to do the work by myself? Tell her to help me!'"

In modern language, Martha was trying to lay a guilt trip on both Mary and Jesus, Mary for not doing her duty and Jesus for not reminding her of that fact. Guilt feelings are a part of almost everyone's daily life. Many people would agree with Paul Tournier that "all upbringing is a cultivation of the sense of guilt on an intensive scale," but they might not agree that daily life is seasoned by a guilty conscience.[1]

What exactly is guilt? It seems as though almost every writer on the subject has a different definition, explanation, or approach. James Knight states that although generally guilt is broken down into two types, real guilt and guilt feelings, a clearer grouping would encompass three areas: (1) real guilt, (2) neurotic guilt, and (3) existential guilt.

He feels that real guilt comes after wrongdoing, which is accepted as such by the doer who seeks forgiveness and makes restitution. It is a conscious acceptance of deeds committed. Neurotic guilt has roots deep in the unconscious mind and cannot be eliminated through atonement. The intent is equated with the deed and the person reacts as though the misdeed were already accomplished. The person may unconsciously consider wrong what he or she wishes to do and the rituals to atone are endless because relief cannot come, for the wishes continue even though the deeds are never committed.

Existential guilt, which Knight feels is a part of the very structure of being human, is the failure to live up to potentials and failure in interpersonal relationships. This occurs because no one reaches goals, either personally or relationally. It is not a product of parental or cultural prohibitions but of the ability to stand off and look at oneself and reflect on one's choices. Existential guilt is different from neurotic guilt, for it can produce greater creativity in the use of one's own potentials and increased sensitivity in relationships.[2]

Bruce Narramore and Bill Counts' explanation of guilt partly resembles Knight's explanation of existential guilt. They believe that guilt feelings come when thoughts or behavior falls short of ideals. Shortly after birth, goals, ideals, and aspirations are developed, which are encouraged by parents and unique to each family. Personal ideals are also influenced by environment (e.g., neighborhoods, schools, peers, television). Narramore and Counts refer to this set of goals as the "ideal-self," firmly established by adolescence. There is also another force shaping a person's deepest self; Narramore and Counts call it a universal awareness of basic moral standards. They feel that every society has an innate sense of right and wrong that silently judges each person's deeds as part of his or her ideal-self.[3]

John Drakeford feels that guilt is commonly thought of, on the one hand, as an unrelenting and tyrannical force that creates misery and unhappiness and, on the other hand, as the stimulus that causes a child to gradually learn the limits of life and the imperatives necessary to become a healthy adult. A sense of guilt is even more important in a person's role in a society that relies on individual conscience as a means of social control. Without this sense of guilt a society would deteriorate.[4]

A differentiation needs to be made between guilt and shame. Guilt is saying, "I *did* wrong." It is a violation of a standard. Shame is saying, "I *am* wrong," a feeling that the individual is a bad, or unacceptable, person. Arthur Becker indicates that shame involves an individual's awareness of others and what they think about him or her, whereas guilt involves the individual's feelings about himself or herself. Both are forms of anxiety deeply involved with one's sense of who one is and who one ought to be. Both guilt and shame, then, have relational aspects but guilt is experienced only in relationships characterized by love or respect. "Guilt feelings signal that something is wrong, not just within one's own soul, but especially in relationships with other persons and with God himself. Guilt feelings signal that we have endangered, weakened, or fractured a relationship important to us."

Becker further states that one type of guilt comes from the effect on a person of an action that is destructive to relationships. The awareness of the act causes guilt feelings that consist of both dread and longing. The dread of separation, loneliness, and alienation causes an anxious longing for reconciliation and restoration of love. Guilt can be the force motivating one toward wholeness and healing or toward despair and destruction. When longing and dread are in proper balance, guilt functions creatively, leading to open and honest recognition of transgression. A sense of hope for forgiveness and restoration results with a willingness to accept forgiveness.

Features of destructive guilt are the inability or unwillingness to recognize personal responsibility, self-vindication often taking the form of self-punishment, loss of hope for forgiveness, and despair. Shifting responsibility to someone else can be used to evade feelings of guilt. Guilt feelings can also be repressed. Though hidden and subconscious, they are a potent force within the person and find avenues of expression often in subtly disguised forms. Becker likens them to boiling water in a tightly covered teakettle with a cork in the spout. When the steam cannot find a normal outlet, it will be released through a flaw in the seam or under the lid. The fire is a person's sense of values or justice or the reality of moral law itself. Whenever the individual hears anything that brings to memory the violation of that law, memories are heated and the steam of guilt tries to escape. The form of escape can be creative and helpful or destructive.

Guilt is also closely linked to conscience, which Becker considers to be the inherited capacity to judge ourselves and our behavior. The standards of the judgment are learned from "significant others" from the moment of birth and are the product of personal relations.[5] Drakeford represents conscience as a wholesome and creative aspect of personality that helps individuals achieve their highest possibilities.[6] This could be referred to as self-monitoring behavior.

Knight states that conscience represents inner controls that enable human beings to distinguish right from wrong, to act upon the right, and to refrain from doing wrong. He considers this the faculty an individual uses to pass judgment on his or her own acts and to bring about atonement and restitution.[7]

Tournier separates true guilt from false guilt. True guilt results when a person feels reproached by God in his or her innermost heart; false guilt results from human judgments, such as social taboos or the fear of losing the love of others.[8] While everyone suffers some secret guilt because of the judgment of others, the healthy person will be able to justify his or her own actions and continue functioning normally. Missionaries are particularly susceptible to guilt, not because of misdeeds but because of the good not done.

False guilt can also involve individuals' concepts of God, of His will for their lives. This may come from inappropriately interpreting the Bible, of blaming self when self has committed no wrong. False guilt can also come from taking responsibility for someone else's misdeeds or misfortune when they are not the individual's fault, such as a child's blaming himself or herself for the parents' divorce.

Tournier also distinguishes between repressed guilt, which leads to anger, rebellion, fear and anxiety, a deadening of conscience, an inability to recognize faults and aggressive tendencies; and recognized guilt, which results in repentance, a sense of peace and security of divine pardon, a refined conscience, and a weakening of aggressive impulses.[9]

Narramore and Counts feel that three attitudes form the core of guilt emotions: a fear of punishment, a sense of unworthiness, and the fear of rejection.[10] Guilt feelings result when thoughts or behavior falls short of ideals. If sins are hidden, the individual will be plagued with various forms of guilt. If they are acknowledged, the person will be forgiven and experience peace and reconciliation. "Since guilt is a painful feeling, we unknowingly disguise it and hide it from our conscious minds. By pushing it into the unconscious, we think we're free. But our restless emotional lives betray us."[11]

Why, then, do some people continue to feel bad even after they have asked for forgiveness? It may be because they continue to live with shame, the feeling they are less than perfect, flawed in some way because they committed the misdeed. They consider others who have never committed such acts as better than themselves and look on themselves as second-class citizens.

Missionaries seem particularly inclined to several of the reactions to feelings of guilt mentioned by Narramore and Counts. They may repress feelings of pleasure because of a sense of constant duty or they may blame themselves when others are at fault. They may find difficulty in saying no, even when loaded down with responsibilities, for fear of disapproval. Some become critics who avoid looking at their own faults by focusing on those of others. While some are motivated by guilt to act, others are paralyzed.

Caryll Houselander suggests that an outstanding characteristic of feelings of guilt is its inconsistency. Some who lead blameless lives are overwhelmed by a sense of guilt, while others who lead guilty lives may be devoid of it. Often the more a person does wrong, the less he or she recognizes it as wrongdoing. Most people feel guilty because they *are* guilty, but if the individual is unable or unwilling to cope with the cause of the guilt, neurosis or morbidity may result. Also, the true cause of the guilt feelings may be dislocated. Houselander likens this phenomenon to a person who suffers from cancer seeking desperately for some other explanation for the symptoms.[12]

Confession has already been mentioned as a method of overcoming guilt feelings. Although used through the centuries by the Catholic Church, confession to a pastor or priest on a regular basis for continued fellowship with the church has not been a part of Protestantism. Public confession during church services or prayer meetings, although less in practice today, was a part of early fundamental evangelical and Pentecostal denominations. During periods of spiritual revival in Bible colleges, when classes would be canceled so that students could continue to seek God's face, many students would spontaneously confess to cheating, lying, and stealing before the entire student body.[13]

Missionaries could probably be helped with their feelings of guilt if they could confess to or be counseled by a competent professional.[14] The counselor could help missionaries distinguish between real and neurotic guilt. They could help the individuals isolate the action and discover why they felt it was wrong. Because of their leadership roles, it would be extremely difficult for missionaries to confess publicly in services in the host country or to the leadership of the national church. Unfortunately, field directors have often had the difficult task of explaining the faults of repatriated missionaries to these very people when situations have deteriorated.

Besides confession, Knight has detailed several other mechanisms of dissipating guilt. Reparation is a constructive method by which the individual makes amends for the damage. Punishment, the destructive opposite of reparation, may work with reparation in rehabilitation. The person, suffering from guilt, feels better after punishment for his or her conduct. Rationalization is the substitution of socially acceptable reasons for actions rather than seeing them objectively. Projection is assigning one's own traits and motives to another or attaching the guilt to a substitute object if the cause cannot be identified. In the Garden of Eden, Adam blamed Eve, Eve blamed the serpent, and the serpent blamed God. Adolf Hitler blamed the Jews for provoking the Second World War. Sympathy is a feeling of suffering with, and a wish to help, a person who is suffering pain, loss, defeat, or misfortune. Feelings of guilt, inadequacy, and worthlessness may disappear as the person gives himself or herself to alleviate the suffering of others. As an illustration of sympathy, Knight used the example of housewives of businessmen in Colombia who were showing neurotic symptoms because they had servants to do all their housework. They felt useless and guilty until they became involved in social work, helping the unfortunate.[15]

There are specific areas of overseas ministry that can be potential causes of guilt for missionaries.

DEALING WITH LIVING STANDARDS

The problem of the housewives in Colombia is generally one

of the first problems of guilt faced by the new missionary. "What right do I have to live in a comfortable, modern house when the host people are living in shacks or huts?" (Some of these problems were mentioned in chapter 4.) If the mission board has a policy that designates where and how the missionary will live, the guilt can be dissipated through projection: "I am only following policy." In older, established missions where mission compounds were first built, both missionaries and national church leaders may now be living in the same type of house on the compounds. Since many of these institutions have been turned over to national church organizations, missionaries have little or no say as to where they will live.

However, another problem arises when properties are given to the national church organization. Who is going to repair and maintain these buildings? Even though the missionary is assigned a house by the church, he or she will almost invariably have more funds to maintain the building than would a national pastor. Should Mr. Missionary paint the walls, cement up the rat holes, and repair the plumbing to keep peace with his family, or should he live in the house as is, facing the consequences of dirt and disease? Or should he give the national church the funds necessary to repair all the church-owned houses (which could lead to a confrontation with fellow missionaries)?

Harriet Hill, who did her best to live exactly as the host people in a rural village in order to become a cultural insider, found that she failed miserably.

Even after years of trying, vast differences remained. The model that sounded so wonderful in my missions classes wasn't working for me, but rather than question the model, I assumed the problem was myself. I was doing something wrong, I was failing God, and guilt overwhelmed me. Not only that, my children also suffered because when they needed stability, I was frantically changing things to achieve an incarnational ministry.[16]

Jon Bonk identifies three aspects of the affluence problem: the standard of living, the use of high-tech equipment, and the lack of social contact with host people. His thesis is that all missionaries should live simply, like the incarnational model. (See chapter 4, "Bonding.") Stan Nussbaum, in replying to Bonk, suggests that rich missionaries *can* have poor friends and that these very friendships can provide incentives for a simpler lifestyle. James Plueddmann suggests that the issue is not affluence, but love. Affluent missionaries planted one of the fastest-growing churches in the world in Africa. Placing a load of guilt on missionaries because of their lifestyle does not help their ministry. Many of them are already living simply by Western standards. Love is the key to friendships and relationships—not living standards.[17]

Neither Jesus nor Paul seemed to advocate a one-class system. In Colossians 3:22, Paul instructs slaves to obey their earthly masters in everything, not to seek freedom, and Jesus said we would have the poor with us always (Matt. 26:11).

As more and more new missionaries are sent to large, modern cities where they live in the same type of accommodations as middle- and upper-income nationals, living standards become less of an issue. A young couple went to Kinshasa, Zaire, prepared for an incarnational ministry and ready to bond with a host family. While working in a large evangelical church, they became very friendly with several host young people who invited them home for a meal. Imagine the shock to this jeans-and-T-shirt-clad couple when a chauffeur-driven limousine came to take them to their friends' home, a mansion by anyone's standard!

In dealing with the problem of living standards, each individual missionary or couple needs to ask the following questions:

Why is it necessary for me to live like this?

What effect is this lifestyle having on my emotional well-being?

Does my lifestyle have any effect on my ministry?

Would the host people accept my having a different standard of living if it would mean more years of service as a missionary?

DEALING WITH SUFFERING

It is almost impossible to pick up a newspaper or to listen to a newscast today without seeing or hearing about the suffering in the world. As soon as a famine is over in one country, it is reported in some other part of the world. Religious and secular magazines bombard the individual with appeals for donations for relief. Besides religious organizations that are geared solely to relief, almost every denomination has a department set up to handle such situations. Missionaries are being sent constantly to work among political and economic refugees.

Guilt felt by missionaries seldom has to do with global suffering, for relief organizations address such situations. But what should I do about the beggars I meet everyday on each street corner? What do I do about the pastor who needs money for his wife's operation or his children's schooling? How much help should I give to a Bible school student who can't pay his or her fees?

By Western standards, the vast majority of the people missionaries work with are suffering. Because missionaries are trained, nurturing, caring people who believe that giving is part of loving, who want to follow the example of the Good Samaritan (Luke 10:25–37), they will naturally feel an obligation to help.

It isn't long, though, until they are inundated with requests. If a beggar receives help once, he will expect to receive help on a regular basis. In a small town in central Africa, a missionary gave help to a beggar. The next time the beggar saw the woman, he followed her all around town shouting obscenities because she refused to help him again.

There are no pat answers or easy solutions to the problem. No missionary is immune to some feelings of guilt when confronted with the deprivation of those around him or her. If some on the field are more generous than others, conflicts will arise among the missionaries as well as with the national church. When firm policies are established by the sending organization with the cooperation of the national church, many conflicts can be avoided. Some national church organizations and local churches have their own methods of helping those with desperate needs. The leaders in one national church told all the missionaries that they were never to loan or give money to national pastors but that if they saw someone in need, they could refer him or her to the church committee.[18]

Missionaries also must learn to see needs as the host people see them. In many developing countries, if a person has food, clothing, and some sort of shelter, he is not considered in need. The host country may make a totally different distinction between essential and nonessential from what the missionary would. When Jesus said that we would always have the poor with us, He did not offer a standard for determining who qualifies for assistance.

DEALING WITH CHILDREN'S EDUCATION

One of the major reasons missionaries give for leaving the field is their children's education,[19] despite the fact that the number of options for education on the field is greater than ever and growing constantly. Home study programs have been refined to include computer programs and videotapes. Sending workbooks and tests away for correction is no longer necessary. International schools are available in most large cities where education follows Western standards and classes are taught in English. Mission-run boarding schools are available in every part of the third world, many with a standard of education exceeding that of the majority of public schools in the United States.[20]

Missionary children are an integral part of their parents' ministry. Ted Ward points out that neglect of family is not part of God's call on an individual's life. He does not ask missionaries to dichotomize their responsibilities along the lines of ministry versus family. Ward suggests that new missionaries today, because of a negative view of the intercultural experience, feel that the overseas experience during childhood and adolescence will hurt their children. All these matters need to be discussed before the family leaves for the field.[21]

Most mission agencies allow missionaries to choose whatever method they consider best. However, having options does not necessarily alleviate anxiety. Those opting for home schooling have to deal with priorities of responsibility—work versus family. Because the mother will have to do the majority of the teaching or supervising, the question of her competency has to be considered. Paul Nelson feels that the temperaments of the mother and the children influence success far more than high motivation and good materials. Also there is the knowledge that the children need to be with peers to learn social skills.[22]

Unless the mission board has a fixed policy concerning children's education, flexibility in a candidate's attitude about schooling is an important factor. In a number of evangelical circles home schooling has become a crusade, both in the United States and overseas. Extensive seminars are given to parents to prepare them for the home-schooling experience. Children are

**CHAPTER
8**

**Dealing
With
Guilt**

considered the exclusive responsibility of the parents and to neglect this responsibility is a sin. One couple with this attitude arrived on the field with two teenagers, one first-grader, and a new baby. Although the mother was qualified and the older children well motivated, after a few months it became evident that the family needed help. A short-term couple came to the field especially to teach the children. By the time they arrived, the two older children had asked to go to boarding school, which they were permitted to do and where they adjusted with no major problems. However, the father stated publicly that he felt he was sinning by sending his children to boarding school and at the end of their first term transferred to another field that would not require doing so.

In referring to flexibility, David Pollock states that the emotional and personal needs of both children and parents must be considered. Administrators should be sensitive to people who have strong opinions about the milieu their children are developed and educated in. All the alternatives need to be viewed not as sources of conflict but as opportunities for the satisfactory development of missionary children.[23]

Although home-schooling materials are constantly being updated to make the task easier and less time-consuming for parents, advocates would probably agree with Nelson's opinion that this should be considered a short-term option. Each child's current needs should be individually evaluated. Families should cope with the situation a year at a time while evaluating all available options. Positive parental attitudes about all the possibilities will usually engender positive responses from the children. David Wickstrom and J. Roland Fleck in a study of self-esteem and dependency among missionary children in college concluded that self-esteem was related to family relationships. Children who saw their parents as warm and accepting and who were not subject to guilt-inducing control seemed to have a higher degree of self-esteem. Pollock suggests that parents' expectations may need to be altered so that they can understand that the "third-culture" experience is a positive, healthy one that will prepare their children for their future role in an internationalized world.[24]

Ted Ward, who has done extensive research on missionary children's schooling, found that children would make the best of whatever available schooling if the family was strong and the members committed to each other without being overly protective or compulsively dominating. The children, raised in a bicultural situation, will probably develop social skills, interpersonal sensitivity, and linguistic ability beyond their cousins in North America. In the modern world, there is greater demand for interculturally and linguistically experienced young people in government service and business endeavors as well as in missionary service.

It is Ward's opinion that mission boards should offer parent-skills workshops, as well as appropriate parenting literature to missionaries. Missionary parents also need well-formed support networks. Many of the problems that occur among missionary children would occur wherever the family was located. The bicultural or multicultural experience has been found to be a positive feature for most children. Problems are generally not caused by the overseas experience but by conflicts within the family itself.[25]

Some missionaries opt to send their children to a local school, especially those trying to follow the incarnational method of bonding with the host people. The parents have the advantage of the children's living at home and the children the advantage of becoming intimately acquainted with another culture as well as becoming bilingual. Cost is minimal. One danger is that the child risks ending up with no internalized culture. White feels that this method of education should be considered only if the parents plan to stay permanently in the host country. Otherwise the child is faced with the task of constantly rearranging and reintegrating the values, philosophies, relationships, and behaviors of the two cultures.[26]

Another critical factor in missionary children's education is curriculum. Pollock considers any mode of education inadequate if it fails to satisfy educational criteria, even though it may meet the requirements of theology, child growth and development, parental emotional demands, and ministry standards. He feels that mission boards need to produce an educational curriculum that will permit reasonable ease in transition to home countries, while at the same time promoting an intercultural worldview.[27]

There are pros and cons to any method of overseas education.[28] Each child in each family is different. One child may adjust well to boarding school while another child in the same family may have difficulty. One child may adapt well to home schooling, being motivated to advance as quickly as possible, while another needs the structure of a classroom. One family who had spent their first two terms in a large city where their children went to an international school transferred to the interior of the country for their third term. They were very excited about home schooling their children who were now teenagers. However, after only a few months, they decided to send the children to a mission boarding school in the area. The girl adjusted well but the boy had problems, both scholastically and socially. The parents then found a more advanced home study method, which they used successfully for the rest of the term.

Larry Sharp did a study of 268 adults who as children of missionaries to Brazil had had five years of boarding experience; he compared them to 262 adults who had no boarding experience. Although not necessarily advocating boarding school for all children, he came to the following conclusions:

1. The boarding school concept does not in itself produce detrimental effects. Problems are generally caused because of the child's personality, attitudes of the parents, houseparents not suited for the job, or unresolved conflicts within the child.
2. Parental attitude is probably the biggest factor in the child's adjustment to boarding school. If the parents are not convinced that this is the best way and have not prepared themselves and their children, problems will result.
3. Husband-wife as well as parent-child relationships are the key to adjustment. The child is prepared to exit and reenter the family successfully when the relationship between the parents is loving and stable.
4. Although parental separation from children is not easy, it can be the right solution for some children and for some families. Sharp found that for most children the boarding school experience produces a positive, well-adjusted young person.
5. Missionary children themselves said that the advantages far outweigh the disadvantages—98.1 percent of the 268 adults who had boarding school experiences, from a number of different mission backgrounds, indicated that they would choose the same experience again.[29]

Another issue seldom addressed is the training of house-parents. It seems that a number of mission boards rely on volunteers for the position instead of actively recruiting those with experience and training in the field. In one instance, the children rebelled so strongly against their dorm parents that the missionaries on the field took immediate action. The couple in question was removed from the school and parents took turns running the hostel until permanent houseparents could be found. These missionaries, realizing the importance of the position, were willing to take a year out of their busy schedules to become surrogate parents to children far from home.

Pollock suggests special intercultural courses in Christian colleges to train students anticipating cross-cultural vocations as teachers and dorm parents.[30] Prefield orientation programs could also include specialized sessions for those interested in being dorm parents. Some psychological testing is probably important. One couple was sent out on an emergency basis because of the sudden death of the former houseparent. They had been preparing to go to another field but felt definitely led to accept the position when they heard of the situation, even though they were inadequately funded. However, it soon became clear to the other missionaries on the field that the couple were not prepared for the pressure of being responsible for children from a number of different denominational backgrounds. Coming from a conservative background themselves, they took exception to certain typical teenage hairstyles, jewelry, and modes of dress. This rigidity of attitude could probably have been detected with proper testing, thus preventing a tense situation at the school before they returned prematurely to the United States, after only a few months of service.

Several mission boards, such as the Christian and Missionary Alliance, require their missionaries to send their children to boarding school. Although the pain of separation will be felt, guilt feelings will be minimized because the decision was accepted before coming to the field. However, all missionaries need to keep in mind that family unity is based on something deeper than geographical location.[31] Loving concern sometimes has to go beyond the barrier of the fear of separation. Children's education is as big a problem in many places in the United States as it is in second or third world countries.

DEALING WITH AGING PARENTS

Although research is scarce on the care of older parents, such care is a problem facing an increasing number of missionaries, especially those who are an only child. Married siblings of single women missionaries sometimes expect them to care for their widowed mother. In some cases, retired parents can join their child on the mission field, finding some type of work to keep themselves occupied. On one field, the retired parents ran the guest house and on another where the father was a qualified mechanic, the couple set up a repair shop for mission vehicles.

Of course, this solution is seldom possible if the parents are disabled. Placing a parent in a nursing home is a very traumatic experience for people living in the United States even when they will be able to visit the parent regularly. For those who know they will be separated for long periods of time it is doubly hard.

Finances are also a consideration. Few missionaries are in a financial position to pay the high cost of nursing home care unless the parent qualifies for government help. One couple, after three terms on the mission field and with a very effective ministry in Bible school work, remained in the States to care for the husband's partially disabled mother. They had made arrangements to place her in a nursing home when they discovered that her income would not cover the costs. With their own children in high school and college, they were not able to cover her additional expenses and made arrangements for her to stay with them instead.

This problem usually occurs when missionaries are having their most effective ministry in the host country. They have generally learned a language, made necessary adjustments to the culture, found fulfillment in their work, and worked through their children's educational difficulties. In many cases, their children are already functioning on their own. When mission agencies have flexible policies on furloughs, allowing missionaries more frequent visits to the States, some of the anxiety can be alleviated. Since emphasis in the past has been placed on how to solve missionary children's problems (and rightly so), some concern should now be shown for missionaries' problems with aging parents.

DEALING WITH CIVIL AUTHORITY

Far more than their peers at home, missionaries have to deal with all three types of guilt mentioned by Narramore and Counts: civil, theological, and psychological.

Civil or legal guilt results from the violation of human law.[32] Living in countries where governments are often corrupt and laws are made for the enrichment of the lawmakers, missionaries are constantly faced with the problem of having to adjust to the local value system to get anything accomplished. Solving the difference between a bribe and a gratuity can cause some deep-seated anxiety. In a number of third world countries, if a person is accidentally hit by a car, the mob will kill the driver. It is extremely difficult for a missionary to drive off to the nearest police station or to the embassy, leaving an injured person lying on the street.

In one instance, a missionary hit a young girl who ran suddenly out of a crowd into the path of the car. The first instinct for the husband was to stop, but his wife screamed at him to continue driving. Since they were headed to the airport, they continued to the home of an army colonel who was in charge of airport security and who attended their church. The army officer kept their car, so that it would not be recognized by those who witnessed the accident, and sent them home in his own limousine. This kind friend also promised to take care of any legal problems. Both the missionaries were extremely traumatized by the incident, especially the wife, who was a nurse and could have given expert care to the child. The week before, a government minister had been badly beaten and his chauffeur killed at the same place when they had accidentally killed a child.

One night a missionary with his wife and three children, along with a national pastor and his wife and baby, was on his way to the building site of a new church when he ran into a slow-moving (perhaps parked), unlighted, heavily loaded farm trailer. The disastrous accident resulted in the deaths of all the children and a permanent injury to the missionary's wife. Although clearly not the missionary's fault, he was found guilty by the government and had to pay all the resultant penalties. Because of their firm faith in a loving Heavenly Father, along with the constant support of friends and their mission board, the couple were able to work through their grief and guilt and continued to be effective missionaries for many years. But they

CHAPTER 8

──

Dealing With Guilt

had to be willing to subject themselves to unjust (by American standards) civil law.

Theological guilt results from the violation of divine law.[33] The vast majority of missionaries have settled the question of theological guilt long before arriving on their field of service. In most cases, their reason for coming to the host country is to help the host people find the solution to theological guilt through faith in Christ.

Psychological guilt, according to Narramore, results from a feeling of failure,[34] a feeling missionaries are especially susceptible to because of the constant pressures they work under. Perhaps it would be well for all missionaries to have printed in large letters and placed conspicuously in every room in their home these words of Paul: "'There is therefore now no condemnation for those who are in Christ Jesus.'—Romans 8:1."

Robert McGee considers guilt probably the most destructive emotion, because it causes a loss of self-respect, causes the human spirit to wither, and erodes personal significance. Because guilt plays on fears of failure and rejection, it can never build, encourage, or inspire positive action.[35] Identifying the source of and dealing with feelings of guilt should be a major concern of mission agencies in their efforts to help missionaries have enduring, effective, and rewarding ministries. During orientation programs, special workshops on dealing with guilt would probably help candidates prepare for some of the guilt-producing situations they will face. Also, they should be required to read significant books dealing with guilt and shame.[36] If a qualified counselor was available on a full-time basis, he or she could probably help troubled personnel work through their times of anxiety due to feelings of guilt.

──────────

[1]Paul Tournier, *Guilt and Grace: A Psychological Study* (New York: Harper & Row, 1962), 10.

[2]James A. Knight, *Conscience and Guilt* (New York: Appleton-Century-Crofts, 1969), 91–92.

[3]Bruce Narramore and Bill Counts, *Guilt and Freedom* (Santa Ana, Calif.: Vision House Publishers, 1974), 20–21.

[4]John W. Drakeford, *Integrity Therapy* (Nashville: Broadman Press, 1967), 32–33.

[5]Arthur H. Becker, *Guilt: Curse or Blessing?* (Minneapolis: Augsburg Publishing House, 1977), 14–33, 40.

[6]Drakeford, *Integrity Therapy*, 14.

[7]Knight, *Conscience and Guilt*, 3.

[8]Tournier, *Guilt and Grace*, 63–76.

[9]Ibid., 152.

[10]Narramore and Counts, *Guilt and Freedom*, 19.

[11]Ibid., 8.

[12]Caryll Houselander, *Guilt* (New York: Sheed & Ward, 1951), 1–2, 13.

[13]The author experienced several such confession services at Wheaton College and Central Bible College.

[14]Marge Jones, "First-Year Counseling: A Key Ingredient to Success," *Evangelical Missions Quarterly* 29 (July 1993): 294–98.

[15]Knight, *Conscience and Guilt*, 116–21.

[16]Harriet Hill, "Incarnational Ministry: A Critical Examination," *Evangelical Missions Quarterly* 26 (April 1990): 196–201.

[17]Jon Bonk, "Affluence: The Achilles' Heel of Missions," *Evangelical Missions Quarterly* 21 (October 1985): 383–90; Stan Nussbaum, "Relationships May Precede Economic Adjustments," *Evangelical Missions Quarterly* 21 (October 1985): 390–91; James E. Plueddmann, "The Issue Is Love, Not Affluence," *Evangelical Missions Quarterly* 21 (October 1985): 392–93.

[18]From the author's missionary experience in Zaire, March 1980–May 1990.

[19]K. Lewis, "Creative Concerns for Important Kids," *In Other Words* 9, no. 8 (1983): 1.

[20]For more information contact the Association of Christian Schools International, P. O. Box 4097, Whittier, CA 90607-4097.

[21]Ted Ward, "The Anxious Climate of Concern for Missionary Children," *International Bulletin of Missionary Research* 13, no. 1 (January 1989): 11–13.

[22]Paul Nelson, "Home Schooling in the Missions Context," *Evangelical Missions Quarterly* 24 (April 1988): 126–29.

[23]David C. Pollock, "Strategies for Dealing with Crisis in Missionary Kid Education," *International Bulletin of Missionary Research* 13, no. 1 (January 1989): 14–19.

[24]David Lee Wickstrom and J. Roland Fleck, "Missionary Children: Correlates of Self-esteem and Dependency," *Journal of Psychology and Theology* 11 (Fall 1983): 226–35; Pollock, "Strategies," 13–19.

[25]Ward, "Anxious Climate," 11–13.

[26]Frances J. White, "Some Reflections on the Separation Phenomenon Idiosyncratic to the Experience of Missionaries and Their Children," *Journal of Psychology and Theology* 11 (Fall 1983): 181–88.

[27]Pollock, "Strategies," 13–19.

[28]For a list of pros and cons consult Pollock's article "Strategies," 18–19.

[29]Larry Sharp, "Boarding Schools: What Difference Do They Make?" *Evangelical Missions Quarterly* 26 (January 1990): 26–35.

[30]Pollock, "Strategies," 13–19.

[31]For further studies consult Kelly S. O'Donnell and Michele Lewis O'Donnell, eds., "Educating Missionary Children" in *Helping Missionaries Grow: Readings in Mental Health and Missions* (Pasadena, Calif.: William Carey Library, 1988), 258–301.

[32]Narramore and Counts, *Guilt and Freedom*, 34.

[33]Ibid.

[34]Ibid.

[35]Robert S. McGee, *The Search for Significance*, 2d ed. (Houston, Tex.: Rapha Publishing, 1990), 166.

[36]For example, John Bradshaw, *Healing the Shame That Binds You* (Deerfield Beach, Fla.: Health Communications, 1988).

Chapter Nine

Conflicts

"On that day a great persecution broke out against the church at Jerusalem, and all except the apostles were scattered. . . . Those who had been scattered preached the word wherever they went" (Acts 8:1,4). Missions was birthed in conflict. The established religious body, Judaism, was having problems with a bunch of radicals who were preaching that the Messiah had come. Unfortunately, this heresy was gaining thousands of adherents in Jerusalem. So the leaders decided to put out the fire by persecuting the followers. This persecution had exactly the opposite effect. It spread the fire and started the first great wave of missionary evangelism.

The apostle Paul, perhaps the greatest missionary who ever lived, certainly had his share of conflict. Right after his conversion and his call to the mission field, his own Jewish people tried to kill him. To make matters worse, the leaders of the embryonic "denomination," which he wanted to join, didn't want anything to do with him. Fortunately Barnabas, the "son of encouragement," took a chance on this reactionary and gave him all the proper introductions (Acts 9:23–27).

Paul's next conflict came with the very man who had gained him acceptance in the church. After a very successful missionary tour, he had a strong disagreement with Barnabas about the advisability of giving a young recruit a second chance after he

**CHAPTER
9**
——
Conflicts

had washed out the first time. In fact, the disagreement was so strong the two colleagues decided to split, with the net result of having the missionary task force from the Antioch church doubled (Acts 15:36–41).

Even before this, a doctrinal dispute had to be settled with "headquarters." Since no definitive statement of the fundamentals of faith had been established, some men from the home church in Jerusalem started teaching a different opinion about the method of salvation than that preached by Paul. A council had to be convened, all parties heard, a decision reached by a word of wisdom from the Holy Spirit, and the resolution sent out (Acts 15:1–33).

Conflicts are just as much a part of missionary work today as they were in Paul's day. Disagreement with the home board, difficulties with fellow missionaries, and problems with the national church are part of the daily pressures encountered on the mission field. How these conflicts are faced and resolved will determine the effectiveness and duration of an individual's career overseas.

Conflict With the Mission Board

"That is not what the resolution said!" A group of missionaries were discussing the distribution of their contributions to various departments at headquarters with the field representative. "Yes, but all of you know that your intention was for the funds to go to Bro. John Doe and not for running the office. So we have been sending all the money to him each month, as you intended," was the adamant reply. As the discussion heated up, it became apparent that no solution would be reached at that meeting. The head office continued to support the individual in question while the field continued to send fax messages and other correspondence asking that the contributions be used in other areas.

Stan Smith (pseudonym for a missionary who served in Zaire for more than twenty-five years) found the following to be problems he encountered with his mission board:

1. "Home staff see missionaries as the means to enlarging the home end. Missionaries see home staff as the means for doing their work on the field. Each uses the other." The home staff's emphasis is on raising prayer and financial support from church-

es while missionaries feel that their work should be the focal point because they are fulfilling the Great Commission.

2. "Home-end planners do not seek and heed missionaries' counsel." This is very evident in the feeling of the missionaries in the above example. The home board feels that it sees the larger picture, planning for a global strategy with an objective outlook, while missionaries are viewed as being "sentimentally fixed on their own little area or project." This attitude can lead to a lack of consultation with field missionaries, who may have a much broader view than generally accepted.

3. "Home staff have financial advantages over field missionaries." Differences in personal income can become a barrier to effective collaboration. Executives may have spouses who work while this is impossible for field missionaries because of local work restrictions, their heavy workload in the ministry, or mission policy.

4. "Home staff criticize missionaries for not 'going native.'" Some mission executives may insist that their field missionaries live a very simple lifestyle, as close as possible to that of the majority in the host country, forgetting the pressures this may bring to the individual or family involved. Their lack of comprehension of the harassments of overseas living can lead to poor relationships.

5. "Home executives impose unrealistic workloads on missionaries." According to Smith, in spite of incorporation of personnel management techniques from business into church organizations, missionary job satisfaction has not noticeably improved. Excessive workloads and nonproductive paperwork are not appreciated. Smith states that Protestant organizations could do well to emulate Roman Catholic policy, which has strictly-limited responsibilities for each missionary and compulsory daily and periodic rest periods for spiritual renewal in their own cultural milieu. Smith feels that "the destabilizing psychological influences of constant exposure to an unpredictable and often twisted foreign culture are more devastating than armchair theoreticians may believe."

6. "Visits by home executives are too rushed. Pastoral care is lacking." Missionaries become frustrated if, after months of unanswered questions, long postal delays, and repeated crises, the visit from home office personnel is too short. Often there is so much information about home office decisions to transmit

that there is not enough time for personal visits with each individual missionary. Pastoral care for ministers at the home base seems to be more important than pastoral care for missionaries.

7. "Recruitment and screening of candidates are ineffective." The home office, because of budgetary restrictions, may be limiting the number of candidates accepted even though the workload of field missionaries is increasing. On the other hand, sometimes field missionaries feel that the home board accepts almost anyone who can raise the necessary funds, without adequately screening his or her ability to function on the field.

8. "Home executives are out of tune with the basic purpose of missions." Missionaries sent out by some mainline denominations (those affiliated with the World Council of Churches, such as Methodists, Lutherans, and Presbyterians) may have a much more evangelical outlook than their home office. For example, mission agency executives may be chosen for their management techniques rather than for their dedication to Jesus Christ.

9. "Under orders from the home office, missionaries are subservient to churches in 'receiving' countries." Because local national church leadership may not have the same goals as the missionaries, they may find themselves working under very frustrating circumstances.[1]

The two areas of greatest concern to the missionaries were rushed visits by home executives and lack of pastoral care. These were followed closely by ineffective recruitment and screening of candidates and lack of consultation with the field on decisions affecting them. Frank Allen feels that a leading cause of friction between leaders and missionaries is North American individualism, which leads to neither good teamwork nor recognition of authority. The words "The Lord is leading me" could easily cause friction as well as havoc with field programs if the individual's "leading" is contrary to that felt by the majority of the group.[2]

Smith offers a number of solutions for the above problems. He suggests that the sending agency should accept its role as the support base for the missionaries, who are doing the real work of missions. The home office needs to do more listening than pronouncing, especially concerning difficult decisions. Salary scales should be as nearly equivalent as possible and an attitude of tolerance should be exhibited toward living conditions and cultural integration. To avoid overloads, job descriptions should be given to local church authorities as well as to missionaries.

Groups from the home churches should be encouraged to participate in work projects on the field, especially where language comprehension is not required. This would alleviate some of the pressure on the local missionary as well as achieve a greater participation of those supporting the missionary endeavor. Visits by the home staff should be long enough to adequately treat the problems facing field personnel. If the personality of the executive discourages rather than encourages confidences, perhaps visits by special people chosen for their gifts of pastoral care could be provided.

A constant review of the recruitment, screening, and orientation process would probably help to provide the type of workers needed on an ever-changing mission field. Mission boards need to listen to their personnel who are on the field and know the frontline needs. The relationship between missionaries whose theology is more evangelical than that of their home board cannot be easily resolved; each missionary will have to decide whether he or she can function under such circumstances. It may be that the church in the host country is more evangelical than the denomination it originated from. A great deal of flexibility may be needed to resolve differences of opinion between missionaries and the national church[3] (refer to the section "Conflict with National Church Leadership" in this chapter).

The home office needs to remember that candidates are seldom spiritually mature enough to handle a limitless amount of stress. They are people in process, as Myron Loss points out, so the home board needs to exercise patience while the Lord continues their development. Rather than trying to recruit better and better candidates, which don't exist, boards need to recognize that the vast majority of those chosen *are* capable of having a victorious ministry and just need adequate training and support.[4]

Dr. Marjory Foyle gives the following suggestions to help solve administration/personnel conflicts:

1. Constitutions and personnel policies should be clearly written and reviewed often.
2. Rules should leave room for individual decisions. . . . Personnel

policies should be written in such a way that workable alternatives are evident and people's preferences are respected.
3. Communication channels between administration and personnel should be carefully designed and implemented to allow for free flow in both directions.
4. Personnel should love, cherish, and respect their administrator—which implies that he or she is fit for the job.
5. Administrators should have training in management.[5]

Kenneth Gangel, in discussing the development of new leadership, suggests that decision making and authority should be pushed as far as possible down the ranks so that the people actually involved have the major voice in the decision. This decentralization would pull together a group of leaders who share responsibility for decisions and the outcome of those decisions. It means "keeping administrators out of policy making and board members out of policy implementation. Decentralization means crucifying personal rights and authority for the good of the mission and advancement of the body of Christ."[6]

Missionary personnel also need to be aware of the pressures on the administrators. Field and regional directors generally have a heavy travel schedule, constantly changing time zones and work schedules. They are often faced with a different problem at every stop. They have to juggle the expectations of the home constituency with the problems of individual missionaries, field policies, and national church interests. Often they also have the responsibility of raising funds for mission projects and then seeing to the equable distribution of the funds. Those chosen for their administrative abilities may be inadequately prepared for their counseling duties; those who have the ability to raise funds for projects may have difficulty communicating adequately with national church leaders.

Pastoral care for administrators is just as important as pastoral care for field missionaries. Division and delineation of responsibilities is important both for the mental health of the administrator and for the progress of the work on the field with the least amount of stress. Administrators who are under pressure because of heavy workloads may find it difficult to treat field problems with patience and understanding.

CONFLICT WITH OTHER MISSIONARIES

Two new couples were sent by one mission board as their first missionaries to open a new field. Both couples felt called to this country and were excited about the work. Each had two children similar in age, all four adults had master's degrees in Bible or missions and were fluent in the local official language. After studying the tribal language, both couples seemed to have bonded well with the nationals, enjoyed local food, visited village churches, encouraged visits from the national pastors, and helped them register their organization with the national government.

The duties of each couple were delineated after they had been on the field for a year and had had a chance to see the needs. One couple decided to help a young pastor start a new church in a community where there was no Christian witness and the other started a Bible training program for young men who felt called to the ministry. To all intents and purposes, this seemed to be an ideal team.

But by the time the first couple came home on furlough, a serious rift had developed. Bill (not his real name) was an action person. He had no problem coming to a quick decision and carrying it out. He formed quick opinions that were hard to change. He had a tendency to be outspoken, with the result that his quiet, more thoughtful wife would have to try to soften some of his statements. His wife, talented and capable, taught the children as well as ably handled household duties. Because finances were not a problem, they had full-time household help. Bill was a very strict disciplinarian.

Dave (not his real name), on the other hand, was a much more quiet, introverted person who had to think every situation through thoroughly before coming to a decision. Even after making a decision, he would have trouble implementing it without several consultations with the home office. It was very difficult for him to confront anyone and he would often have headaches if conflicts arose. His wife, an able administrator, was active in the Bible training program and handled all necessary financial reports. Because they were able to afford only part-time help, Dave often helped with the cooking, which he thoroughly enjoyed, as well as other household duties.

Both Bill and Dave seemed to have an open and warm relationship with the local pastors. Both families adjusted to the culture, developing a genuine love for the people they were working with. Both saw results from their ministry although they were working in a country where Christianity had made little progress. What, then, caused the serious rift in their relationships?

Dr. Foyle, after a number of years of dealing with missionary relationship problems, refers to personality immaturity as a leading cause of friction. Traits such as "difficulty in trusting others, inferiority, boastfulness or overdogmatism, overdramatization of events and a tendency to exaggerate, persistent jealousy, and the persistence of other negative emotions" should be noted during the screening process. She gives the following suggestions for dealing with such negative attitudes, especially in situations where professional help is not available.

1. Instead of brooding about a problem, commit it to God, for He is always ready to help.
2. Ask God to help you find the basis for the attitude and then look for Bible passages that specifically deal with your feelings.
3. Others may be unconscious of causing distress so it is necessary to try to understand why they behave toward you as they do. They also have problems to deal with.
4. Practice creative forgiveness by forgiving the debtor as well as the debt, or the act that has hurt you.[7]

One source of conflict for new missionaries can be trying to work in harmony with older missionaries. Often newcomers have unrealistic expectations of those with more experience on the field. They may expect them to be spiritual giants, have a fluency in the local language, have a good working relationship with the national church leaders, and be able to give detailed instruction on how to cope with culture shock.

The veteran missionary, on the other hand, may be wary of the new recruit, fearing that his or her own shortcomings will become painfully evident. The new missionaries may then be perceived as a threat to established relationships and routines. Foyle observes that new missionaries, "who are smart and well trained, often see what is wrong very quickly—but instead of trying to understand why things are as they are, and approaching the matter tactfully, they rush in prematurely with suggestions." Older workers tend to become defensive when criticized.[8]

If veteran missionaries could understand the traits that facilitate acceptance of the new generation, listed by Allen, tension would likely be lessened. New recruits expect their leaders to

1. be models in all of life: spiritually, physically, and mentally;
2. be good communicators;
3. be flexible enough to entertain new ideas;
4. be open to new ways of doing things;
5. be able to resolve personal conflicts and solve problems;
6. be able teachers;
7. be able to shepherd and nurture others;
8. seek the growth and success of those they lead;
9. be servants, first of all;
10. be willing to train younger leaders;
11. be experienced team leaders;
12. be understanding of the new generation;
13. be sensitive to potential conflict that new workers face;
14. be willing to sacrifice personal ambition for the sake of helping younger missionaries;
15. help with supervised goal planning.[9]

On one mission field that had a reputation for losing new missionaries at the end of one term, the national church leaders asked the mission board to please send out older missionaries who were already used to living under more difficult situations. Two couples arrived on the field at the same time, one a veteran of twenty years and the other a novice. It soon became evident that the new couple wanted no advice or help from the older couple. After their first term this couple resigned and another new couple was sent out. The veteran missionaries, after making them as comfortable as possible, left them strictly on their own, knowing that the national church would soon have them involved in ministry. After only a few months on the field, the new recruits wrote to the head office that they were having problems because they were not given adequate direction!

Myron Loss suggests several ways that senior missionaries can help new recruits:

1. Give them measurable and attainable goals.
2. Don't be threatened by the arrival of new workers.
3. Don't underestimate the stress of culture change.

4. Take a vacation.
5. Treat new workers as equals.
6. Believe in people.

Loss feels that veteran missionaries have a decisive influence on the future of new workers. Their attitude, whether positive or negative, will usually be passed down to the younger missionaries. Veterans need to maintain a healthy self-esteem to become good communicators and establish a close friendship with their junior fellow workers.[10]

In a survey of 549 missionaries, Dorothy Gish found that confronting others when necessary is the greatest source of stress for a majority of missionaries. She feels that on-site, in-service training would be helpful, such as workshops where the individual would have to practice conflict resolution skills with fellow workers.[11]

Helen Herndon warns about the effect of unresolved chronic problems on the field. She feels that "it takes less effort to label situations as 'personality conflicts' than as 'sin,'" thus aimlessly chopping at the fruit of the problems rather than at their root.

It is not rare to find missionaries persecuting missionaries. Such cruelty and lack of love from "within" have disillusioned many a young, zealous, and idealistic worker. Missionaries are human, fallible beings belonging to human, fallible organizations. But the fact that we are Christians and Christian organizations should supersede the former condition.[12]

Some conflicts are more uniquely confronted by women on the mission field. Single women are often encouraged or forced to have a female coworker by their mission board. If the women are permitted to choose their own partner, they will generally choose a colleague with the same interests and lifestyle. When personalities mesh and there is a shared burden for the ministry they are engaged in, a long and fulfilling relationship can be the result. However, if the personalities and working styles are not compatible, conflict may well result. Frances White suggests that a coworker who cannot relate in a healthy manner can be more frustrating than having no fellow worker to meet intimacy needs.[13]

Conflicts can also arise when the professional qualifications of women are ignored by male-dominated structures and attitudes. Herndon states that women often feel unappreciated by fellow missionaries and leaders, both professionally and as people.[14] In one organization, missionary wives who did the work of a treasurer were not made members of the field committee, but if a man did the same job, he was.

One area seldom addressed is the conflict that can arise between missionaries from different countries and cultures who have to work together. As national churches gain independence from the parent organization, they often invite professionals from different countries. Third world countries are now sending missionaries, as well. Foyle,[15] who worked in a hospital with professionals from several European and Asian countries, notes four areas where difficulties can arise.

Language. Expatriates (those people who are not citizens of the host country) will generally converse in one of the major languages of the world, usually the officially recognized national language, even if the majority of the people use trade or tribal languages. This language may not be the mother tongue for many of the missionaries and words can often be used incorrectly, causing offense. Lack of fluency and faulty pronunciation can inhibit timid missionaries who may become more withdrawn, causing a breakdown in cooperation.

Working patterns. Missionaries bring their home-country work ethic and patterns with them to the host country. It is natural that they would continue to use the system they are familiar with. Workable compromises need to be agreed upon even for such simple things as using feet or meters in construction and Fahrenheit or centigrade for taking temperatures.

Social and cultural customs. In several French-speaking countries of Africa, controversy arose between the missionaries about the correct way to serve Communion. French missionaries were adamant that using one cup was the biblical method while American missionaries insisted on individual cups because of hygiene. The use of wine or grape juice caused even more friction. Each of the missionaries advocated their method and used it in the area they were working in. When the national churches were organized with their own leadership, they would decide on which method to use. Missionaries were then forced to use the method adopted by the national church leadership.

Sandra Mackin suggests that most of the cultural conflicts

**CHAPTER
9**
―――――
Conflicts

between multinational team members revolve around practices that are not clearly defined in the Bible. She feels that team leaders should hold a seminar during which teammates can become acquainted with each other's culture. It is important that leadership styles and decision-making strategies be understood by all. Samuel Chiang gives the following suggestions for a smooth working policy:

1. All members need to agree on doctrine and ethical behavior.
2. They should share a common goal.
3. Open communication is important.
4. They need to demonstrate trust and accountability.
5. They must pray for each other.[16]

Conflicts can also arise about the role of women in the church. Several evangelical European churches do not allow women to have any leadership positions. They practice and teach the letter of the law found in Paul's message to Timothy, "I do not permit a woman to teach or to have authority over a man; she must be silent" (1 Tim. 2:12). Certain dress codes are also advocated and often followed even after a national church has been organized. Generally American missionaries have difficulty conforming to these codes and have a tendency to teach their own ideas whenever given an opportunity.

One missionary couple, both of whom had theological training and were ordained, transferred from a country where the wife was used in a teaching ministry to another where she was not allowed to do so. Being fluent in the language and a trained biblical teacher, she became very frustrated after a short time. They did not complete one term on that field. In another country, a veteran missionary couple, both the husband and wife, were asked by national church pastors to hold a seminar. When the French missionaries heard that the wife was going to participate, they refused to cooperate in the seminar and excommunicated all the national pastors who participated.

Financial disparity. Not only do salaries vary greatly between missionaries coming from different countries, but so does their access to equipment, as well as relief and project funds. Most nationals feel that all expatriates are rich, no matter their home country. Now that third world countries are also sending missionaries, who tend to live more as the host country pastors do, the disparity is even greater. The Canadian government as well as a number of European governments channel their aid through missionaries.[17] Sharp disagreement can arise about the distribution of these funds or supplies.

A strong national church organization with a set standard of conduct is often the only solution to expatriate conflict. Candidates who tend to be less flexible in their beliefs should generally not be sent into situations where they will have to work closely with missionaries from other cultures. Orientation programs need to deal with the possibility of this type of conflict when discussing culture shock.

Dr. Laura Mae Gardner, after a study of terminations from the Wycliffe Bible Translators, offered a number of recommendations for the proactive care of missionary personnel. She found that communication problems were a source of termination at all levels—between marriage partners, among family members, between the family and field colleagues, between the worker and the administration, and between the worker and his home constituency. She recommends that mission leaders and workers should learn techniques of appropriate confrontation. She agrees with Gish that an administrator is often tempted to avoid a problem, transfer the problem person to another department, or pass the situation to a successor, rather than confront. Reluctance to confront may result in "manipulative behavior, gossip, and other unproductive ways of coping with problems."[18]

Conflict With Family Members

Although family problems have been mentioned as a leading cause of missionary attrition, such problems are generally due to education or health—not internal conflicts. Conflicts between parents and children are probably fewer among missionary families than among any similar group in North America. Several factors likely contribute to this. Missionary home situations are generally stable, the children receiving quality support.[19] Many prefield orientation programs now have special training programs for children in conjunction with the adult candidate programs. In addition, specialized departments to handle MK needs have been incorporated into a number of mission organizations.

Missionary children are part of a unique culture made up of

both the host country and the home country. Rather than a deprivation, this can be an advantage, for the child is often comfortable in diverse cultures and situations. Larry Sharp found that generally MKs are honest, submissive, highly intelligent, and emotionally stable. Rather than finding their being rebellious toward their parents, Downes reports that 90 percent of MKs surveyed listed their parents as their best friends.[20] In another survey, 95 percent of MKs said they would choose to be an MK, if they could "do it again."[21]

Besides mentioning the normal child/parent conflict areas, Foyle notes several that are more unique to the mission field. Missionaries often do not have the funds to provide different hobbies considered normal in the same social milieu in North America.[22] Conflicts can occur if the child feels disadvantaged when returning to the home country.

Most MKs have the advantage of a loving, supportive missionary community as well as a stable home situation. They are also encouraged to integrate the local culture with their home culture, thus becoming part of a "third culture," which is "neither North American nor foreign but an amalgamation that is quite different from the sum of its parts."[23] However, conflicts can arise when the child has to face the problem of preserving relationships with local friends while avoiding those cultural expectations that are not compatible with family values.

Living in an Islamic country raises the dilemma of social freedom for missionary girls, since local custom forbids the mixing of the sexes; MKs may become frustrated and bored after the freedom they have enjoyed in a boarding school situation. Foyle suggests taking holidays in a less restrictive atmosphere and joining an embassy club, where sports facilities as well as a number of other activities are available under reasonable adult supervision.[24]

In many third world countries, missionaries are very reluctant to see relationships between their children and nationals develop into a commitment that may lead to marriage. Parents are generally more aware of the problems the couple will face because of ingrained cultural differences, which are not apparent to the children. High-school-aged young people who are sent to boarding schools will be more apt to form attachments with peers from their own cultural backgrounds than those young people who live with their parents.

In the past, MKs were often sent to Christian academies in North America for their high school education. Separation from parents at this critical age may have caused a number of problems, such as feeling abandoned, but it did allow them the opportunity to bond with young people from their own cultural and religious backgrounds. No statistics are available about the number of missionaries who may have left the field, either temporarily or permanently, because of this problem.

One missionary couple left the field early, ostensibly because of physical problems. Actually, the principal reason was probably because their daughter fell in love with the son of a family in the local church pastored by the missionary. The young man, a strong Christian with a good education, was from a mixed European-African background. He continued his biblical education, obtaining a good position at the American embassy in a neighboring country, where he started several churches and eventually became a leader in the national church organization. His parents, still solid leaders in their home church, find it difficult to understand why their son was not considered worthy to be accepted into this missionary family.

Dr. Foyle[25] has listed five different areas of stress for missionary families that can lead to conflict. The first is the goldfish bowl effect (treated in a previous chapter). Missionaries, like many of their counterparts in Western societies, feel that part of their ministry is to show biblical principles through their marriage and family relationships. Therefore, problems affecting these relationships may produce guilt because of a perceived failure of Christian witness as well as because of the difficulties themselves. The feeling of being constantly scrutinized by curious national neighbors can lead to frustration and may exacerbate any interpersonal family difficulties. Missionary couples need to understand what is happening and come to terms with the guilt they are feeling. The quality of the marriage is the important factor, not the "news bulletins" produced by domestic help!

Vocation is a second source of conflict. Both partners should feel called to the mission field. If either spouse agrees to go to the field simply to fulfill the other's call, the marriage and their future ministry could be in serious trouble. Wives and husbands should be interviewed separately as well as together. However, wives may be very reluctant to talk openly to an all-male committee. Dr. Foyle noted that a number of candidate wives who kept very quiet when meeting with the committee opened up to her in private.

Missionary appointments are generally made on the basis of the husband's ministry. Many wives feel they will be satisfied with their roles as helper and mother, especially if they plan to home school their children. They may find this fulfilling as long as the children are with them. If, however, it becomes apparent that the children need to go to boarding school for cultural, interpersonal, or educational reasons, their mothers may find themselves with a lot of time and little to do. Wives need to feel that they are just as much a part of the missionary team as their husbands and have a meaningful ministry role whether or not they have had the same professional training.

Dr. Foyle noted two cases where the appointment was made because of the wife's ministry and the husbands accepted their position as a challenge. This is a rare occurrence, thus showing the progressive attitude of the mission board. If the husband has a good measure of self-confidence and self-esteem with no ego problem, he will probably be able to accept a wife with an acclaimed ministry, vicariously taking part in her accomplishments. In one large African city, a missionary husband and wife were copastors of a growing international church. Her ministry was just as much appreciated as his. At a well-known mission hospital, the wife was the chief surgeon while the husband, with no medical training, was in charge of construction. Their marriage was considered one of the happiest at the mission station in spite of her long hours and strenuous work schedule.

Working in an Islamic social structure can also cause stress leading to conflict. Although single women working in schools or hospitals may be accepted as social enigmas, married women are expected to behave as Muslim wives do, not coming out of their homes to be seen in public. Some missionary wives working under these conditions have reported a rewarding ministry among Muslim women. Any couple planning to work under these conditions will need a firm understanding of the limitations the wife will face.

Many mission boards make provision for and encourage male missionaries in continuing their education while on furlough. Single women can also often seize the opportunity to do so, since they do not have the domestic responsibilities of their married counterparts. Wives and mothers, on the other hand, usually have to wait until they are older (when learning can be more difficult) to get the added education that would have helped their ministry years before.

A number of years ago one missionary couple decided to live in a city where the wife could obtain a master's degree in her field during their second furlough. Besides keeping house for three elementary school children, working part-time as a secretary to help pay for her education, and itinerating many weekends, she obtained her degree fifteen months later and was accepted into a doctoral program. Although her mission board was permitting two other male missionaries to continue their furloughs to work in a doctoral program, she was never given the opportunity to do so. However, the mission board now always takes into account her professional qualifications as well as her husband's when considering their overseas assignment.

Marital and sexual stresses leading to friction certainly aren't unique to missionary couples. The number of missionary divorces is probably considerably lower than the national American average. However, Foyle points out several conditions that are often unique to the mission field.

Lack of privacy can cause problems. During language school, accommodations can be cramped and inadequate, with fellow students living too close for comfort. When finally established on the field, the couple may find that walls are thin, doors do not lock, and neighbors are constantly in and out. The couple may need to establish a routine of privacy, finding culturally acceptable ways of locking out the public for regular times of intimacy.

In some cultures, it is not socially acceptable for a husband to show affection to his wife in public, thus robbing the couple of signs of love that have become meaningful to their marriage. Both husband and wife will need to decide just how much adjustment needs to be made to these patterns of restraint. One older missionary couple decided that pastors in their area needed to learn to show more affection, for their cultural mores were causing more harm than good in protecting marriages. They not only showed public affection but also held seminars with the pastors on marriage relationships. Pastors and their wives thanked the couple for bringing more joy and love into their marriage. Marriage enrichment and family seminars are often asked for by national pastors.

Personality differences can be more stressful on the mission field simply because the couple tends to spend more time together than they normally would under similar circumstances in America. The husband's office may well be in the home. In a mission compound, the hospital, church, or school is generally within walking distance of the home. Husbands and wives may well be working together, allowing personality clashes to become very visible.

In a comprehensive article on resolving conflicts in Christian marriages, Kenneth Williams lists the following steps as necessary commitments and ground rules:

1. You have a problem and take it to God. Take a good look at the problem to see if it is serious or trivial.
2. Bring up the issue with your partner, asking when would be a good time to discuss the problem.
3. Explain your problem and how you feel about it.
4. Propose a tentative solution that could be mutually satisfactory.
5. Let your partner respond. Your partner may agree, disagree completely, or suggest an alternate solution. If an agreement is reached, it should be clearly stated and the problem resolved.
6. Take an intermission if a solution isn't reached quickly. Allow time for prayer and healing, asking God to give the wisdom needed to find a solution that will bring joy to both partners.
7. Ask for and grant forgiveness. This does not imply that either of you were wrong but that you want your spouse to be free from hurt and resentment so that your relationship may be restored.
8. Review the situation to see what God would have you learn from it. If both of you are not happy with the solution, seek help from an outside source.[26]

Several Christian mental-health clinics have been established especially to deal with unresolved individual, familial, and marital conflicts. Christian family counselors are readily available in America, and more and more mission boards are requiring con-

flicted families to get professional help. Saving a missionary
marriage or resolving a family conflict is well worth the effort—
even at considerable cost.

CONFLICT WITH NATIONAL CHURCH LEADERSHIP

Since missionaries during the past one hundred years have
accomplished the task of establishing sovereign, local church
organizations in many third world countries, the modern candidate often works in cooperation with or under the direction of a
local bishop, church president, pastor, or elder. Conflicts can
occur in several areas as a result.

The placement of the missionary can become a touchy point.
Often because of family considerations, the missionary may not
want to live where the church organization feels he is needed.
One national church badly needed missionaries to work in their
largest Bible school with almost two hundred students.
However, the school was located in a very remote area where the
supplies the family would need were not available. Also,
although the road to the regional capital had at one time been
maintained, the government no longer did so. The result is that
the trip which used to take three hours now took at least twelve.
After a meeting between the leaders and missionaries, it was
decided that one missionary couple would try to spend two
months each year at the school, teaching a concentration of
needed courses. Missionaries living in the busy, noisy city often
tried to find time to escape to the isolated quiet of the school,
where they were treated like visiting royalty!

If possible, the question of missionary placement needs to be
agreed upon before the missionary arrives on the field. But no
amount of orientation can adequately prepare the candidate for
the actuality of the situation he or she will be living in. If it is a
question of the missionary leaving the field or moving to another area, national church leadership would probably choose the
latter. Open communication of the reasons behind the need for
transfer is of vital importance. Bishops, presidents, presbyters,
pastors, and laity are often very sensitive to the needs of their
foreign coworkers.

Job descriptions can also be a source of conflict. Nationals
may feel that the missionary, simply because of his or her superi-
or education, has an unlimited supply of talent in a variety of

fields. The precedent set by former missionaries who, because of necessity, often built buildings, repaired vehicles, grew large gardens as well as teaching in the Bible school and preaching weekends, may lead to unrealistic expectations.

In addition, if the national church has a specific need, they may ask the missionary to fill it, whether or not he or she came to the field for that purpose. In one instance, the bishop insisted that the missionary run the finances of the diocese even though he came to teach in the seminary. The missionary did not return to that situation after furlough.

Perhaps the likeliest area of potential conflict between the national church and missionaries is finance. As leadership in the church is transferred from missionaries to nationals, theoretically so is financial responsibility. The methods of financing or not financing national pastors and organizations are almost as prolific as mission agencies. Although many churches have been established on indigenous principles—self-supporting, self-propagating, and self-governing[27]—very few of them actually operate with no foreign aid of any kind.

If a firm policy has been established between the mission agency and the independent national church, the missionary can refer to the policy when approached for funds. There always have been and always will be those nationals who will leave one church for another for financial reasons. Probably one of the greatest disappointments a missionary can have is to see a promising young pastor who has been trained and nurtured for a number of years decide to minister in another church organization for financial gain.

Even though policies for funding have been established and agreed upon, the interpretation of those policies is often left to individual missionaries. When project funds have been depleted, nationals often feel that somehow the source can provide more. National church organizations are simply following the leadership of their third world governments in considering Western countries as an unlimited source for finances. Missionaries who insist that there are no more funds can be seen as being indifferent to the needs of the church. Visiting preachers from America, seeing the desperate need in some countries, often have a tendency to pledge funds that may not agree with local missionary or national church policy. Again the missionary may find himself between two conflicting opinions.

In one African country, the national church accused the missionaries of not releasing funds sent for them. The missionaries then had to prove that the home church had never sent the funds. A warm working relationship which had grown in trust and confidence was nearly severed. A number of missions now send funds directly to national church organizations. The missionary, then, is no longer involved in the distribution or use of the funds. But the missionary is involved in the outcome of the use of the funds. If the funds that were sent to build a clinic go instead to renovate the bishop's house, the missionary still finds himself in the middle of a controversy.

Missionaries working in the same organization may have differing views of how much help should be given the church. Although a policy had long been established on one field of not giving to individual pastors, several missionaries continued to give from personal funds if a crisis arose. They felt that they had a right to give if so led of the Lord. This not only caused a division between the missionaries, but also brought a deep rift between the national church leadership and the missionary who held to the letter of the law. Eventually there had to be a change in missionary personnel for the situation to be resolved.

There are no easy solutions to national church and missionary conflicts. Where there is mutual respect and trust there will be fewer conflicts. When missionaries and nationals work together in all areas of the church, including that of finances, some friction can probably be avoided. In some third world countries, national churches have developed economically to the place where no outside funds are needed. Not only are they supplying the finances for all their own departments and projects, they also are sending missionaries to neighboring countries.

---

[1]Stan Smith, "The Trouble with My Home Board Is . . . ," *Evangelical Missions Quarterly* 21 (April 1985): 118–28.

[2]Frank Allen, "Why Do They Leave? Reflections on Attrition," *Evangelical Missions Quarterly* 22 (April 1986): 118–28.

[3]Smith, "The Trouble," 125–28.

[4]Myron Loss, *Culture Shock: Dealing with Stress in Cross-Cultural Living* (Winona Lake, Ind.: Light and Life Press, 1983), 79.

[5]Marjory Foyle, "Missionary Relationships: Powderkeg or Powerhouse?" *Evangelical Missions Quarterly* 21 (October 1985): 342–49.

[6]Kenneth O. Gangel, "Developing New Leaders for the Global Task," *Evangelical Missions Quarterly* 25 (April 1989): 166–71.

[7]Marjory Foyle, "Gorillas Get Along: Why Can't We?" *Evangelical Missions Quarterly* 22 (January 1986): 14–20.

[8]Marjory Foyle, "Why It's Tough to Get Along with Each Other," *Evangelical Missions Quarterly* 21 (July 1985): 240–45.

[9]Frank Allen, "Making Room for the New Generation," *Evangelical Missions Quarterly* 25 (October 1989): 395–98.

[10]Loss, *Culture Shock*, 103–8.

[11]Dorothy J. Gish, "Sources of Missionary Stress," *Journal of Psychology and Theology* 11 (Fall 1983): 236–42.

[12]Helen Louise Herndon, "How Many 'Dropouts' Really Are 'Pushouts'?" *Evangelical Missions Quarterly* 16 (January 1980): 13–15.

[13]Frances J. White, "Some Reflections on the Separation Phenomenon Idiosyncratic to the Experience of Missionaries and Their Children," *Journal of Psychology and Theology* 11 (Fall 1983): 181–88.

[14]Herndon, "How Many 'Dropouts,'" 13–15.

[15]Foyle, "Missionary Relationships," 342–49.

[16]Sandra L. Mackin, "Multinational Teams: Smooth as Silk or Rough as Rawhide?" *Evangelical Missions Quarterly* 28 (April 1992): 134–40; Samuel E. Chiang, "Partnerships at the Crossroads: Red, Yellow, or Green Light?" *Evangelical Missions Quarterly* 28 (July 1992): 284–89.

[17]The Pentecostal Assemblies of Canada distributes relief supplies obtained from the Canadian government in the fields where the denomination has missionaries.

[18]Laura Mae Gardner, "Proactive Care of Missionary Personnel," *Journal of Psychology and Theology* 15 (Winter 1987): 308–14.

[19]Marjory F. Foyle, *Overcoming Missionary Stress* (Wheaton, Ill.: Evangelical Missions Information Service, 1987), 73.

[20]Larry W. Sharp, "Toward a Greater Understanding of the Real MK: A Review of Recent Research," in *Helping Missionaries Grow: Readings in Mental Health and Missions*, eds. Kelly S. O'Donnell and Michele Lewis O'Donnell (Pasadena, Calif.: William Carey Library, 1988), 219–28; R. F. Downes, "A Look at the Third Culture Child," *The Japan Christian Quarterly* (Spring 1976): 68–71.

[21]Sharp, "The Real MK," 222.

[22]Foyle, *Overcoming Missionary Stress*, 71.

[23]White, "Some Reflections," 181–88.

[24]Foyle, *Overcoming Missionary Stress*, 73–75.

[25]Ibid., 41–50.

[26]Kenneth L. Williams, "Resolving Conflicts in Christian Marriage," in

Helping Missionaries Grow: Readings in Mental Health and Missions, eds. Kelly S. O'Donnell and Michele Lewis O'Donnell (Pasadena, Calif.: William Carey Library, 1988), 211–18.

[27]Summary of Melvin L. Hodges, *The Indigenous Church* (Springfield, Mo.: Gospel Publishing House, 1953).

**CHAPTER
9**

Conflicts

Chapter Ten

Reentry

The longtime missions director of one major evangelical denomination once said that it was harder to get missionaries to retire than to start. The occasion was a panel discussion between veteran missionaries and new candidates during a missionary orientation program. Several of the veterans had spent over forty years on the mission field and were reluctantly making the adjustment to living in the United States again.

A number of years ago, a veteran missionary from Latin America was at home because of his wife's ill health. He had repeatedly asked the mission board to allow him to return to the field but had been refused because of his age, which was well past retirement. When his wife died, he left the body at the mortuary, used the money the board had sent him for her funeral to buy a ticket, and returned to the field! It would be doubtful if this situation could or would happen today. But the problems of reentry into North American culture are probably just as numerous as they were thirty years ago.

Retired

Viewing retirement as a welcome change or as a painful ordeal is certainly not exclusive to missionaries. Many professionals in North America remain in their work well into their seventies and even eighties, continuing to be productive and respected in their fields. The same is probably true for missionaries, although no studies seem to exist on this subject. Missionaries who have spent twenty or more years on the field probably feel far more at home there than they would back in America. They have carved their niche, established their worth, formed long-term friendships, and often don't want their lives interrupted. They would probably rather die and be buried in the host country than make the adjustment back to a Western culture.

There are, however, veteran missionaries who are just waiting until that sixty-fifth birthday to settle back into the luxury of stateside living. They are looking forward to spending more time with family and home-church friends. They may plan trips and vacations which they never before had time to take. One veteran couple, after forty years of service, is thoroughly enjoying using all their free-mileage plane tickets to travel around the world. Another couple, while still involved in their field work, talk constantly about "next year" when they can retire and spend time with their grandchildren. These people have prepared themselves for the transition and are looking forward to it. This may not be the case for many other retirees.

Dr. Marjory Foyle[1] refers to the reentry stress of retiring missionaries as reverse culture shock. Loss of a familiar environment produces a type of bereavement, a mourning for the overseas home they have left behind. They struggle with feelings of insecurity, overemotionalism, loneliness, and a sensation of being lost. Missionaries need to understand that this mourning process is normal, for they have been cut off from much that has become familiar to them. Some may have become so engrossed with their work that they are emotionally dependent on it. Panic attacks, depression, and anxiety can result when they are deprived of their normal activity.

Foyle notes a number of issues that the missionary faces at retirement.

Social and professional status. The individual, after years of position and status in the community, suddenly becomes a nobody. He or she is no longer greeted by almost everyone in the neighborhood. The former missionary's advice is no longer sought by leaders in the community.

Old friends, especially nationals. Veteran missionaries who have adapted to their host country have naturally made lasting friendships with their national colleagues. Often they have pioneered churches together, established Bible training programs, labored together through difficult situations, rejoiced together over victories, and grieved together over losses. Their acceptance and understanding of each other have crossed all cultural barriers. The veteran missionary probably feels much closer to these friends than he or she will ever feel to the new ones in the home country.

Meaningful work. If missionaries have remained overseas for several terms, they have probably experienced real job satisfaction. Its loss can be overwhelming if there is no future opportunity for creative work. G. Dal Congdon suggests that retiring missionaries can be a gold mine for cross-cultural ministry in North America, for they are uniquely qualified to work among minorities. Recently retired veteran missionaries to Taiwan are pioneering a Chinese-language church in Philadelphia. They know the language and culture, have all the necessary Bible training, and have already acquired cross-cultural communication skills. They can also be an invaluable asset in missionary training schools.[2]

After over forty years of overseas work, twenty years of which were spent as a field director, a veteran missionary was forced to retire because of his denomination's policy. He was immediately asked by a Bible college to teach missions courses, which he did for five years, receiving the outstanding teacher award during that time. When the Bible college let him go because of his age, a Christian secular college in the same city invited him to continue his ministry there, which he did for several more years. After that, he was invited by a well-known Christian television ministry to establish a missions program in their short-term Bible training school. Finally his wife persuaded him that they needed a less stressful lifestyle. They moved to a retirement community but it wasn't long until "Uncle Maynard" was involved in prison ministry, writing letters to inmates and traveling to correctional institutions to hold services. Through the course of the next twelve years, thousands of prisoners found a personal friend in this retired missionary, who was still typing letters the week his heart quit beating.[3]

Housing. In the past, missionaries' salaries often were not sufficient to permit those working overseas to invest in a home in North America. Fortunately this situation has changed, allowing many career missionaries to purchase a house during furlough and to rent it during their overseas term, thus building equity in their future residence. Retirement complexes are being provided by a number of mission boards, which are often ideally suited to retired missionaries. Not only are the costs kept to a minimum, but the missionary can have fellowship with old friends and coworkers.

Finances. Dr. Foyle mentions finances as a major source of stress if no retirement plan has been established by the board. Savings plans on some missionary salaries are very difficult. Also, income-level differences between missionaries and their colleagues can have "profound social and professional implications." This is especially true when the missionary's income is compared to that of retired pastors and other church workers in the United States.

Norman Frisbey, in a study of evangelical missionaries, found that there was no significant change in psychological or physical health at retirement. More missionaries considered retirement a blessing rather than a shock. The major factor was learning to cope with a drop in income. Financial resources are of primary importance in the adjustment process.[4]

Ignorance. The proliferation of technical knowledge can be overwhelming to individuals who have spent twenty or thirty years living in conditions that can only be described as primitive. Although missionaries have coped daily with situations that would stump many Americans, they feel completely inhibited when faced with modern electronic equipment. Since electronics have recently invaded many third world nations, at least in the main cities if not in the rest of the country, newer missionaries may not face this dilemma. Satellite television receivers are found from Haiti to Hanoi, bringing the modern world to the most remote parts of civilization.

Helping retired missionaries find solutions to their reentry problems should be part of the policy of every mission sending agency. Impressive bronze plaques given in recognition of thirty years of service may make attractive wall decorations but they can't be used for house payments. A lifetime invested in building God's kingdom overseas will surely be rewarded in heaven—but few missionaries leave for heaven as soon as they retire.

A number of mission boards are now providing special seminars and workshops to help retirees in their reentry process.

Social Security, retirement plans, and medicare programs are explained. Providing investment counseling for missionaries throughout their tenure would probably help in avoiding reentry financial stress.

Continued short-term ministries could also help in adjusting to the retirement process. If the missionaries are not limited physically, they can often be of great help in situations where fields are short-staffed. Replacing furloughed missionaries in Bible school situations, providing bookkeeping and secretarial services, holding seminars for pastors, preaching revival campaigns, acting as translators for building and medical teams from America, are just a few of the many possibilities.

Retired missionaries can also benefit their home churches in visitation and other ministries. Making a special effort to form a new circle of friends can greatly help lessen the grieving process. Probably the most important factor in any ministry or activity provided for the retiree is that he or she continues to feel useful.

Good-bye celebrations on the field before departure, with public acknowledgment of the missionary's accomplishments, can also help with the separation process. Gifts received from national and missionary colleagues have a special meaning and will bring back many fond memories every time they are admired. These celebrations can also be a good time to forgive wrongs and work through misunderstandings.

TERMINATED

Helen Herndon asked a question a few years ago that is still relevant today: How many dropouts really are "pushouts"? Missionaries terminate their overseas service for any number of reasons and not just because they can't adapt to host-country living conditions. Herndon suggests five reasons for missionary pushouts. These include

1. totalitarian leadership that almost usurps the place of God or the Holy Spirit in the missionary's life
2. a lack of financial responsibility on the part of the home church or board
3. unresolved chronic problems on the field that are never dealt with
4. unintentional misconceptions of ministry and use of spiritual gifts

5. a lack of appreciation for professional missionary women in a male-dominated structure[5]

Frank Allen, in a more comprehensive look at missionary attrition, notes the following reasons for leaving the field (besides the normal ones such as health and retirement):

1. *Lack of gifts.* He found that candidates who had never ministered as evangelists and church planters in America wished to do so in a strange culture using a foreign language.

2. *Culture shock.* Candidates, often due to ethnocentricity, refused to accept the changes necessary to adapt to a different culture. Or, many would succumb to "culture fatigue" caused by the continuing adjustment to different ways of doing, thinking, and speaking.

3. *Unfulfilled expectations.* Candidates were not permitted to do the work they expected to do.

4. *Morals.* Although relatively few in number, some do fall into sexual immorality. Temptation is always present because of close contact with other missionaries and nationals. In other cases a sense of loneliness or isolation may lead to problems.

5. *Family problems.* This is probably the major reason for missionary attrition. Problems between parents and children may cause early departure from the field. Problems between spouses may cause emotional tensions in the children. Parents, especially husbands, may be so busy doing the Lord's work that insufficient attention is given to family needs.

6. *Disagreement with the mission board.* Disagreement with mission policies and practices as well as with field leaders was cited.

7. *Language.* Some candidates never acquired the language mastery needed for evangelism and church planting.[6]

Probably every major mission board has conducted its own survey of why missionaries leave the field. The Evangelical Alliance Mission (TEAM) found the following reasons for attrition besides the normal ones:

1. a desire to help their children over the hurdle between high school and college
2. caring for elderly parents
3. chronic overextension due to lack of sufficient funds

4. underproductivity, misconduct, and friction with co-workers

TEAM has taken the following positive steps to try to conserve valuable workers: "(1) the appointment of a full-time supervisor of pastoral care and counseling; (2) training conferences for field administrators on alternating years, covering both their pastoral and administrative roles; (3) more flexible furlough and rest schedules for some high pressure situations, and (4) placement of workers needing extended time home in 'bridging ministries' for two-year periods (usually on loan to another organization)."[7]

The Conservative Baptist Foreign Mission Society found that nearly 50 percent of their missionaries resign for personal concerns. A breakdown of physical or emotional health was first on the list; followed by family problems—particularly concern for children—the nature of the work, including interpersonal conflicts; and problems related to administration.[8]

Dr. Foyle prefers to use the term "brownout" instead of "burnout" for early missionary terminations. Burnout may occur in people who have worked for too long in stressful situations. They cannot be considered burned-out bits of rubbish but individuals who have suffered a loss of voltage because of exhaustion. Brownout may indicate that a good job has been done, and valuable, life-changing lessons can be learned during this period. Restoration is needed, both physical and spiritual.[9]

Dr. Kath Donovan, who had to retire for health reasons after seventeen years of overseas service, suggests the following steps to help the adjustment process:

1. Acknowledge grief.
2. Face present realities. Accept that overseas ministry is no longer possible.
3. Draw a healthy line on the past. As painful as funerals are, they signal not only an end, but also a beginning. One of the most common hindrances to adjustment is the idea that overseas service is best and therefore anything else must be second best.
4. Commit yourself to the present task. "The secret of healthy adjustment to the home situation is to see it as just as much God's calling as the overseas situation was."[10]

One missionary, who had to leave after only a few months on the field because of a serious medical problem, has kept in constant contact with the missions board. He and his wife receive newsletters from many missionaries for whom they pray regularly. They are also on the list of special prayer partners called any time of the day or night to pray for urgent needs. Missionaries are always welcome in the church he pastors. With tears in his eyes, he will tell them, "I can never get away from my call!"

Missionaries who have terminated because of conflict with the mission board may often be bitter. Seldom can they see the situation from a truly objective point of view. The parents' deep-seated hurts are passed on to the children, often causing resentment that may last for years. If reconciliation is to take place, it will generally have to happen before the letter of resignation arrives at the office.

Psychological help when problems first surface may reduce dropouts. Besides TEAM, a number of other mission boards now have full-time professional counselors on staff. Discouraged, disillusioned missionaries need someone who can intervene on their behalf as well as someone nonthreatening to whom they can talk. One mission board appointed area directors who were supposed to act as pastors for the missionaries. However, the directors became so involved in administrative duties that they seldom found the time necessary to spend with individual missionaries.

Laura Mae Gardner feels that responsibility for early termination does not rest on the missionary alone but on every department of the mission board. The candidate department needs to eliminate those candidates having problems that indicate they will probably not be long-term, productive workers. The pre-field training program needs to continue screening candidates as well as providing information and orientation. Placement of workers needs to be considered individually and carefully after a study of the candidate's skills and personality as well as a study of the "personality" of the field. Field administrators need to monitor the candidate's adjustment to working conditions and professional counselors need to be available, on a full-time basis, to meet personal, spiritual, emotional, or relational needs of the missionaries.[11]

In spite of concerted effort on the part of every department, painful terminations are going to occur. Working through the trauma of ruptured relationships will probably take infinite patience on the part of administration personnel. Blame-placing seldom helps in the healing process. The home office is probably going to have to take the initiative in restoring trust; the battle-weary veteran is in no condition to take his or her own temperature.

───────────

[1]Marjory F. Foyle, *Overcoming Missionary Stress* (Wheaton, Ill.: Evangelical Missions Information Service, 1987), 130–31, 137–42.

[2]G. Dal Congdon, "Retiring Missionaries, Gold Mine of Workers for North American Cross-Cultural Ministry," *Evangelical Missions Quarterly* 25 (April 1989): 176–81.

[3]Dr. Maynard Ketcham was father and grandfather to the authors.

[4]Norman Frisbey, "Retirement of Evangelical Missionaries: Elements of Satisfaction and Morale," *Journal of Psychology and Theology* 15 (Winter 1987): 326–35.

[5]Helen Louise Herndon, "How Many 'Dropouts' Really Are 'Pushouts'?" *Evangelical Missions Quarterly* 16 (January 1980): 13–15.

[6]Frank Allen, "Why Do They Leave? Reflections on Attrition," *Evangelical Missions Quarterly* 22 (April 1986): 118–22.

[7]Michael Pocock, "The Evangelical Alliance Mission," *Evangelical Missions Quarterly* 22 (April 1986): 122–25.

[8]Dave Camburn, "The Conservative Baptist Foreign Mission Society," *Evangelical Missions Quarterly* 22 (April 1986): 127–28.

[9]Marjory Foyle, "Burnout or Brownout?" *Evangelical Missions Quarterly* 22 (July 1986): 262–70.

[10]Kath Donovan, "'Beauty for Ashes'—Redeeming Premature Field Departure," *Evangelical Missions Quarterly* 27 (January 1991): 18–22.

[11]Laura Mae Gardner, "Proactive Care of Missionary Personnel," *Evangelical Missions Quarterly* 15 (Winter 1987): 308–14.

Chapter Eleven

Satisfaction

How do you measure missionary job satisfaction? Missionary role model Paul has given us his answer. "I have fought the good fight, I have finished the race, I have kept the faith. Now there is in store for me the crown of righteousness, which the Lord, the righteous Judge, will award to me on that day—and not only to me, but also to all who have longed for his appearing" (2 Tim. 4:7–8).

Paul's satisfaction came from several different accomplishments. First of all, he was diligent in his ministry. It would seem that he considered the mission field a battleground, a hostile environment where he was in constant contact with an enemy. There is no indication that he expected to be appreciated, welcomed, or loved. He was a soldier commissioned to fight, using all the armament at his disposal (Eph. 6:10–18). The ultimate victory was not his responsibility (1 Cor. 15:56–58), but perseverance, no matter the circumstance (2 Cor. 11:23–29), certainly was.

Accomplishing the job he was given to do was also a part of Paul's satisfaction. Running a race implies endurance as well as persistence. It means having a goal in mind and not allowing anything to deter one from attaining that goal—not pain or people or problems, not frustrating relationships (e.g., Barnabas) or conflict with the home board (see Acts 15).

**CHAPTER
11**

Satisfaction

Paul never lost his personal assurance of salvation or his faith in Jesus Christ as the only Savior of the world (1 Tim. 4:9–10). This satisfaction culminated in his assured hope of a reward, not financial or material, but eternal. A crown implies authority, the rights and privileges of a monarchy, membership in a royal family.

Paul's satisfaction came from the knowledge that this was not only his reward but it was also the reward of all those who had listened to his teaching and accepted his message. It is interesting that part of his satisfaction came from having his ministry reviewed by a judge, the perfect Judge, who would take into account every aspect of his ability (or lack thereof) as well as the quirks of his personality.

Probably few missionaries are looking for material gain as part of their job satisfaction or they would never have opted for this ministry. The joy of accomplishment seems to come from a knowledge of having fulfilled a calling. Several retired missionaries, each with over forty years of field experience, were asked to write why they felt satisfied. Here are a couple of their answers:

> Sixty years in missions! I look back and marvel at the patience the Lord has had with me and at the way He has led through the years. . . . When He called me to the mission field, I gave up my dream of being a high school teacher. But He had a teaching job for me far more wonderful: in the church, in Bible school, in seminars all over Latin America, and in writing. . . . Boring work? Not at all! Right now I'm working on Volume 3 [of a church history book]. . . . Of course there have been problems. Life is like that, but the joy of being used of God in some way to meet a need far outweighs them all![1]

> I grew up in South Africa, a son of pioneer missionaries. Travel [to America] was difficult during the war years so I got a job in the gold mines. I had my life's work planned and for nearly seven years worked as an engineer. Then God came into my life with His call. The Holy Spirit powerfully impacted my life with the urgency of reaching the lost. The result was forty-two continuous years of evangelistic ministry to the urban Blacks of South Africa. God's call was definite. It revolutionized my life. Never did we think of changing or leaving. It never left us.[2]

MATURITY AND ACHIEVEMENT

The *Evangelical Missions Quarterly* conducted a survey of several veteran missionaries asking them to list "ten sure steps to success." Karen Dubert, in an analysis of the responses, found that the steps had to do with the missionary himself or herself, not with circumstances, finances, or health. The most important step seemed to be the missionary's relationship with God, which had been developed before leaving for the field and maintained after arrival. A solid, prayerful home church is of vital importance as well as a godly home with contented members.[3]

Longevity on the field is not necessarily a sign of success as measured by productivity. Phil Parshall, drawing from his observations during thirty years of travel on the mission field, estimates that 50 percent of missionaries are underactive relative to their potential, although there is no empirical data to substantiate this figure. He found that missionaries who work in institutions where they have to report to superiors tend to be hyperactive, with generally orderly and fulfilling lives.

He observed that those who did not work in regulated, supervised activities, such as church workers, evangelists, researchers, and language students, were often underachievers, both because of their attitudes and the proliferation of high-tech distractions.

Although missionaries are generally considered highly motivated and hardworking, Parshall suggests that many of them may be lazy and unproductive. After thirty years of overseas ministry, he found that the following factors could contribute to a lack of achievement:

Volunteerism is one attitude that can lead to underachievement, according to Parshall. When missionaries feel unappreciated, unrecognized, and underpaid, they can easily slacken their pace. He suggests that mission agencies should recognize accomplishments, such as advanced degrees and published books and articles, with salary increases. "Whether we like it or not, a person who feels professional and is treated with the dignity due a professional is much more likely to perform well than is someone who is simply regarded as a volunteer."

Unfortunately, the hyperactive missionaries he cites as achievers seldom have the time or extra energy needed to write books and articles. They often work well into the evening at home after a long day spent at the institution. Weekends are taken up with preaching ministry in churches, allowing little or no time off for recreation. (One missionary wife, whose husband was a notorious workaholic, found a way to get him out of the office.

After twenty-five years on the mission field, they invested in a television set and VCR. During furlough, she managed to record a number of John Wayne movies, the only programs he would watch besides football games. Once or twice a week, she would start to play one of these old movies, and, almost invariably, her husband could not resist the temptation to relax and watch with her.)

Accountability is another attitude mentioned by Parshall. Missionaries have a tendency to guard their autonomy, not wanting to submit work reports. Helping missionaries recognize the inadequacy of their performance while still encouraging them in their work would require a great deal of expertise in the field of human relations.

Today, however, *discouragement* seems to be more prevalent than ever before. While not finding any specific reason for this, Parshall found that gloom has settled over many missionaries "like an early morning fog. . . . Their unspoken goal is to put in their time and survive until furlough or retirement."

Because of acts of terrorism and violence, *fear* can also be a detriment to meaningful activity on the mission field. Parshall feels that some missionaries have permitted guarantees of safety to predominate over their desire to preach the gospel. "We can't expect evangelistic success if we sequester ourselves in our mission homes."

Parshall also noted the following distractions as a cause of underproductivity:

Living hassles. The demands of survival can force missionaries away from their ministries.

Computers, video, and television. Technology can be either a useful tool or a major distraction.

Fellowship. Although interaction is needed on the field, too much can become a means of avoiding undesirable tasks. Leaders need to stress the imperative of getting assigned jobs done.

Family. Parshall feels that many missionaries are victims of "family priority overkill." "[I]f family dominates our time, then we need to rethink our call to our work."[4]

It should be noted that the apostle Paul had no family considerations to take up his time and energy. Single missionaries have for generations been following his example and could well be praised for their productiveness. Single female missionaries were pioneers on many fields, opening schools, orphanages, and clinics as well as founding churches. One remote Central African field has a strong, indigenous church today because of the work of several single women who stayed in spite of difficulties while five couples in a row left after only one term.

Dr. Clyde Cook suggests the following to enhance missionary productivity:

Reward productivity. This would be possible only if an equitable way of evaluating productivity could be devised, something extremely difficult to do on the mission field. He suggests a system of management by objectives, where clear goals are enumerated and understood by all involved. Reports would center on the accomplishment of those goals rather than on daily activities.

Select carefully. Candidates need to be chosen for their productivity in a ministry similar to the one they will have on the field. Defining mission objectives will help in the selection process.

Build in accountability. A team approach should be used to encourage productivity. He suggests having an office outside the home, which would be a self-disciplinary tool as well as improving the missionary's standing in the community.[5]

What Dr. Cook does not mention is that the objectives of the national church may not be the same as those of the mission board. A number of organizations today, and their number is growing constantly, do not establish churches but work in cooperation with those already in existence. They provide a service to these churches in fields such as translation, education, transportation, evangelism, and medicine. They offer assistance in specific fields—which the national church can accept or reject.

Missionaries involved in church planting have a different set of objectives. Once these objectives are met—generally the establishment of an independent, nationally recognized, and organized religious body—the missionary is then subject to the leadership of that body. Maturity includes the ability to function under that leadership in a meaningful way. Maturity means having infinite patience with a system that may seem to be slow moving and overly materialistic. Maturity involves flexibility and adaptability to a new set of priorities. This type of maturity is probably vitally important to continued effective overseas ministry.

Millard Sall considers the fruit of the Spirit (Gal. 5:22–23) the true marks of a mature Christian.[6] There is little doubt that if missionaries could manifest love, joy, peace, patience, kindness, goodness, faithfulness, gentleness, and self-control on a daily basis, they would be considered spiritually mature. Most mission boards and national church organizations would probably want the mature missionary to exhibit this fruit while actively engaged in profitable work for the kingdom of God.

MATURITY AND FULFILLMENT

Research indicates that job satisfaction includes far more than the basic ingredients of pay, fringe benefits, working conditions, and job security.[7] Opportunities for autonomy and control, chances for advancement, relationships with supervisors and coworkers, as well as aspects of the work itself (whether interesting or boring), are equally important.

Leif Vaage feels that missionaries need to have a better understanding of themselves as different models to have a sense of fulfillment. First of all, they are a means of cultural exchange, which, as a social virtue, strengthens the future of a group of people, aids its survival, and enhances its existence. Since there are no more "pure" cultures (all have had some contact with outside influences), the attention of the missionary should be focused on the most desirable kinds of change. After viewing the weaknesses and strengths of one's own culture, the missionary will find the first changes probably personal, taking place within.

Second, as a student and explorer, the missionary comes to a greater self-understanding of his or her role in the kingdom of God. The missionary also has the role of reporter, helping the sending culture arrive at a better understanding of the so-called foreign culture. But the missionary's most important role is probably one of solidarity with the people of the host country, caring about others as well as self.[8]

Fulfillment in an ongoing commitment to overseas ministry has to account for the different stages in a missionary's career. The satisfaction of having learned a language with enough skill to communicate will not last if there is no adjustment to living in a different culture. Learning to belong in the host country will have had no long-term benefit if children's schooling problems force early retirement.

One missionary wife reported that she cried for a week each time she sent the children to boarding school. The children never knew until they were adults because the crying always came after they had left. During the time the children were home, only positive reinforcement was given about the advantages of boarding school. This missionary certainly couldn't feel fulfilled in being parted from her children, something she accepted as best for their future. The fulfillment came years later as she watched each of them adjust upon reentry to America, finish their education, find Christian mates and satisfying careers.

Kelly S. O'Donnell suggests that better understanding of the cross-cultural and developmental experiences of mission families could come through a construct known as the "family life cycle." In other words, maturation and satisfaction come as certain developmental tasks are accomplished during each of the following stages:

Unattached young adult. Developmental tasks during this period include experimenting with adult work roles, making adult friendships, and separating emotionally and physically from one's family of origin. Tasks particular to those who are interested in overseas work or are already on the mission field would be exposure to cross-cultural situations, possible short-term ministry, and becoming intimate with a potential spouse who has also prioritized mission work.

Newly married couple. Two important but perhaps competing developmental tasks are taking on spousal roles and bonding to a new culture. An important task is to steer a course between the new culture's expectations of the husband-wife roles and those of the homeland. The marriage needs to be firmly established before the couple leaves for the field.

Family with young children. There is generally increased stress and less marital satisfaction after the birth of the first child. An important task is to find a "family niche," a place where the family can fit into the new culture. Children can often serve as cross-cultural links as friendships are formed with a national family. One task is balancing the need for privacy with the need for contact.[9] Missionary wives often face pressure from a multiplicity of roles because of both domestic and mission-related work. They report experiencing more stress than their husbands during all stages of the family life cycle.[10]

Family with adolescents. There is a need for qualitative changes in relationships between the parents and the adolescents who are becoming more independent. Tasks include the choice of schools, helping the adolescents form relationships with peer groups, and the resolution of midlife career issues for the husband and wife.

Launching children and moving on. A major restructuring of the family system is needed as some members are sent into the adult world. An important developmental task is the integration of the child into the original culture. Trial launches, with the possibility of the child returning to the family system, may be needed. Extended family relationships can help with readjustment as the children try to find their cultural and vocational identity. There is the added task of role adjustments within the marital system with the possibility of more time for mission work.

Family in later life. Tasks during this period include preparing for retirement, dealing with declining health, and adjusting job expectations. Important experiences are grandparenthood and widowhood. Often the older couple continue to invest in the lives of their children and grandchildren. Couples may also have the responsibility of caring for aging parents, which can affect their overseas ministry. Some may consider retirement abroad.

O'Donnell suggests that mission agencies may want to periodically assess the current developmental status of each of their families to provide the support and care needed.[11]

MATURATION AND ENJOYMENT

One recent television commercial featured a close-up of a young man eating a hamburger while reporting with much excitement, "I love this place!" The joy missionaries feel certainly has little to do with what they eat or where they live. Those who have found satisfaction and joy in long years of overseas ministry would probably agree with missionary Paul: "I have learned the secret of being content in any and every situation, whether well fed or hungry, whether living in plenty or in want" (Phil. 4:12)

What does bring joy to missionaries? A husband and wife, who had each lost a spouse on the mission field, then met, married, and continued overseas work, had the following to say:

"The joy of hearing one who has never heard that name before bow and accept Jesus as Savior and Lord. The joy of having real brothers and sisters in Christ, both Indian and missionary, succor me in my hours of need and grief. The joy of having my children experience a rounded international education, free from many of the prejudices to which children brought up in the United States are subjected," wrote the husband.

"Life is full of joys that have come as a direct benefit from being a missionary: being a member of an extended and empathetic family of brothers, sisters, uncles, aunts, and (sometimes) additional kids; the privilege of worldwide travel to exotic (?) places; wonderful cross cultural and cross denominational contacts; experiencing the taste of marvelous foods; all this plus forced flexibility," wrote the wife who wound up with a family of ten children.[12]

Surveys on job satisfaction have shown that there is a spillover effect, with satisfaction in one domain overflowing into other areas.[13] It would seem that missionaries who are satisfied with their ministry will also tend to have a happier marriage, more contented children, and better relationships with coworkers.

Laura Gardner, in noting what mission boards could do to help with maturation and satisfaction, included the following:

1. Have an attitude of commitment to growth, to maturity, and to excellence. Missionaries should be encouraged to read specific books, attend retreats and seminars, take regular vacations, and have regular counseling sessions.
2. Commit themselves to proactive care of missionaries who are important as individuals and not just producers. Individuals should be seen and treated as human beings and not just human doers.
3. Include vocational guidance personnel as part of the mission's administrative structure. Special attention needs to be given to experienced senior members who may be affected by a closedown of field programs and by redeployment.[14]

However, none of the retired missionaries who wrote to the author looked to the home office for help in finding joy and satisfaction in their ministry. Relationships with the people seemed to be of primary importance to them, not living conditions or external circumstances. Here are some more of their testimonies:

A missionary who spent forty-four years on the field wrote that the love of the people she was sent to brought her joy, "the changes in a little girl's life whom we rescued from an alcoholic father (he was taking his baby to sell to Hindu priests) and who later became a Bible woman, seeing a whole village leave idol worship to worship the true and living God, the thought of how many people will be enjoying heaven who otherwise would have been lost."[15]

Another missionary wife wrote the following in her recently published book: "We have always firmly believed, and world events have definitely confirmed, that the training of national pastors is the key to evangelizing the world. . . . After more than thirty years spent as missionaries, we felt a great sense of satisfaction and accomplishment in knowing that there were about 1,500 pastors and church leaders scattered throughout Nigeria, doing a great work for the Lord, in whose training we had a small part. I considered it a privilege and joy to work with some of the most delightful people on God's earth. My own life was enriched as we lived among them and saw how God used them to build His kingdom."[16]

Achievement, fulfillment, enjoyment, all of these can be a part of missionary life. It would seem that rewards are both intrinsic and extrinsic, more eternal than temporal, but certainly very satisfying.

Would they do it again? The following testimony probably expresses the sentiment of many retired missionaries.

"Our years of ministry, especially the nearly forty years in missionary work, have left the sweetest taste in my mouth! 'I being in the way, the Lord led me [Gen. 24:27].' I have been very happy wherever and in whatever conditions that leading of the Lord has taken me. Were I to be given the same opportunity again for a half century of service at home and abroad, I would, without any hesitation whatsoever, commit myself to it again. Only this time I would not need to pray about it! It has been that satisfying and fulfilling!"[17]

---

[1] Louise Jeter Walker, from a letter received by Marge Jones, October 1993, used with permission.

[2] Vernon Pettenger, from a letter received by Marge Jones, October 1993, used with permission.

[3]"The Sure Steps to Success as a Missionary: An Evangelical Missions Quarterly Survey," *Evangelical Missions Quarterly* 25 (April 1989): 156–60; Karen Dubert, "Ten Steps to Success: The Major Themes," *Evangelical Missions Quarterly* 25 (April 1989): 161–63.

[4]Phil Parshall, "Why Some People Are Unproductive," *Evangelical Missions Quarterly* 26 (July 1990): 246–51.

[5]Clyde Cook, "Why the Opportunity for Unproductiveness?" *Evangelical Missions Quarterly* 26 (July 1990): 251–53.

[6]Millard J. Sall, *Faith, Psychology and Christian Maturity* (Grand Rapids: Zondervan Publishing House, 1975), 96.

[7]Richard Schulz and Robert B. Ewen, *Adult Development and Aging* (New York: Macmillan Publishing, 1993), 281.

[8]Leif E. Vaage, "On Being a Missionary: Models of Self-understanding," *Missiology: An International Review* 17 (April 1989): 131–41.

[9]Kelly S. O'Donnell, "Developmental Tasks in the Life Cycle of Mission Families" in *Helping Missionaries Grow: Readings in Mental Health and Missions*, eds. Kelly S. O'Donnell and Michele Lewis O'Donnell (Pasadena, Calif.: William Carey Library, 1988), 148–63.

[10]Raymond M. Chester, "Stress on Missionary Families Living in 'Other Culture' Situations," *Journal of Psychology and Christianity* 2, no. 4 (Winter 1983): 30–37.

[11]O'Donnell, "Developmental Tasks," 148–63.

[12]Harriet and Sydney Bryant, personal testimony given September 1993, used with permission.

[13]Beverly A. Schroeder, *Human Growth and Development* (St. Paul: West Publishing Co., 1992), 439.

[14]Laura Mae Gardner, "Proactive Care of Missionary Personnel," *Journal of Psychology and Theology* 15 (Winter 1987): 313–14.

[15]Gladys Ketcham, from a letter received by Marge Jones, October 1993, used with permission.

[16]Excerpts from Esther R. Cimino, *The Touchstone . . . and Me . . .* (Nixa, Mo.: Robison, 1993).

[17]Ralph Cimino, personal testimony given September 1993, used with permission.

CHAPTER 11

Satisfaction

Appendix:
Case Studies

The following case studies are all taken from the lives of actual missionaries who have quit during their first term or shortly thereafter. All names and places have been changed but the rest of the facts have been reported as authentically as possible. All incidents have been reported from public knowledge and no private files or information has been used except with the written permission of the individuals involved.

These cases are used only to help missions candidates review circumstances that could adversely affect their overseas ministry and are in no way meant to denigrate the people whose lives are being studied. History is studied to learn both from its failures and its successes. Rightly or wrongly, missionary success stories are widely publicized while missionary failures are rapidly hidden away in a locked file cabinet. Veteran missionaries and mission boards are well aware of them but seldom are they studied in missions classes or in orientation courses.

In each of the cases, the following questions need to be asked and discussed:

1. What went wrong?
2. Could the situation have been avoided?
3. Was the problem brought to the attention of leadership? If not, why not?
4. Could anything have been done to save their ministry?

THE BROWNS

Rich and Judy Brown were the ideal missions candidates. Sweethearts since high school, they both felt God's call to missionary work at a young age, were active members of an evangelical church, and were married as soon as he finished Bible college and she finished nursing school. Shortly after their marriage, Rich spent a short two-month term in the area where they planned to go as missionaries.

After a short time of ministry as an assistant in his father's large church, Rich accepted the pastorate of a small, struggling church. Judy worked as a nurse to supplement their meager salary. During this time, the couple had two boys. Both Rich and Judy also took flying lessons, knowing that the interior station to which they felt called was very isolated and all communication with the outside world was through the use of small planes. Both of them did very well with their lessons and received their private pilot licenses.

As soon as he received his ordination, Rich and Judy applied for missionary service, went through the battery of tests, and were accepted as candidates. It seems that there were no personal or ministerial problems noted by any of the district leaders who filled out reference forms. Rich's grades in Bible college had been good even though he had been very active in sports as well as outstation ministry.

As soon as they were accepted as candidates, Rich started deputation to raise the necessary support while Judy continued to make a home for the boys. The couple decided that they would home school their children rather than send them to boarding school and procured all the necessary material for a four-year term. Funds were quickly raised, for Rich was well known in his home district. After nine months of language study, during which time a third son was born, the Brown family arrived at their mission station, full of enthusiasm for their new ministry. A lavish welcome was prepared by the national church leaders.

The Browns had to live for a few weeks with the Judsons, the missionaries they were replacing, for a period of orientation. Rich was taken to visit all the major churches in the area, met all the leaders, and became acquainted with the Bible school students. Although new to mission work, Rich had been appointed director of the advanced Bible school because no one else was available. The only other missionaries on the field were the Cricks, a veteran couple involved in church planting several hundred miles away from the Bible school. Also, Rich had always felt called to Bible school ministry.

The first hint of trouble was expressed by Mrs. Judson, who wondered why the Browns, when they were not at meals or directly involved in learning about the town or the work, stayed in their bedroom most of the time instead of visiting. As soon as the Judsons left, the family seemed to settle into a routine, Judy teaching the boys and Rich actively involved in teaching in the Bible school. The Cricks came up to see if they could help in any way, staying at the guest apartment. Mrs. Crick taught some courses at the Bible school while Mr. Crick visited churches and met with the national church leadership, since he was on the national church committee.

The advanced Bible school, only two years old, was meeting in two small rooms in back of the church administration building. The national church said that they would contribute a large tract of land, which they owned on the other side of the city, for a permanent site for the school. All the necessary legal arrangements were made and Rich started drawing up plans for the buildings; he had been able to raise enough funds for the first classroom and administration building. Jim Crick asked to see the plans, since the decision to build as well as the plans themselves had to be accepted by all members on the field, which at that time consisted of only the Browns and the Cricks.

Rich became quite upset, feeling Jim was interfering in his ministry. He had the habit of writing to his parents almost every day, giving them a detailed report of everything that went on. He wrote to his father that Jim was trying to run the Bible school, a message that was passed on to a district leader who in turn contacted the missions board. Jim received a letter from the missions director, asking about the situation. Although the national church leaders had asked Jim to take charge of the building program because of his years in the country, he decided it would be better to completely back away from any decisions regarding the Bible school, including the building.

To finish the building as quickly as possible, Rich decided to cancel classes the following semester to concentrate on the construction. Two single lady nurses returned from furlough and soon became good friends with Judy. Because it became increasingly difficult to keep up with home schooling, after much painful deliberation Rich and Judy decided to send the two older boys to a mission boarding school just an hour away by small plane. The boys had adjusted well to the mission field and soon did the same at the boarding school, becoming involved in sports as well as all the other available activities. Free from teaching duties, Judy was able to help on a regular basis in the local church clinics as well as taking trips to bush-station clinics. During school vacations, the Browns with the two nurses would often take camping trips together to outlying churches, ministering spiritually as well as medically.

At the end of construction, the students and staff moved with enthusiasm into their spacious new quarters. The two nurses, having both had Bible training along with nursing, were able to help with the teaching duties. The Judsons would come up from time to time for national church committee meetings or field meetings when business had to be discussed. These meetings seemed amicable even when differences of opinion were discussed. There was plenty of time for fun and fellowship along with the business.

After two years of ministry, the Browns announced that they had decided to terminate their missionary work at the end of the term the following year. This came as a total surprise to the others on the field, who immediately asked if there was anything they could do to change their minds. The Browns quickly assured all the missionaries that their decision was completely personal and had nothing to do with missionary relationships. They felt they could not continue to send their boys to boarding school, for they did not feel this separation was right. Also, they were thoroughly disgusted with being constantly bombarded for financial help by pastors. But again they stated that the real reason was completely personal; they felt that they had made a mistake thinking that they had a call to missionary work.

As soon as they had a chance, the Judsons asked the two nurses, with whom they had a very close relationship, what had precipitated the Browns' decision. The women said that Rich had become more and more withdrawn, spending hours in his bedroom reading novels when not teaching classes. During national church business meetings, he would pore over a book catalog and never take part in the discussions. They felt that he missed his two older boys very much. Also, they mentioned another fact that the Judsons didn't know: Rich's father had felt a call years earlier to this same country and had put in his application. But because of his wife's health, they had never been able to fulfill their call. However, Rich's parents had been able to come out for Christmas and spend several weeks with the family.

The national church leadership had a big feast for the Browns' farewell, with many long speeches telling them how much their ministry had been appreciated and what a wonderful legacy they had left. Both Rich and Judy were in tears, stating that they wanted to come back for short-term assignments whenever they could get away from their duties in the States. As soon as they arrived back in the States, Judy started working again as a nurse while Rich finished the necessary courses for a master's degree.

But the couple were not content. They could not get away from the call they had felt as young people. After a year, they wrote again to the mission board, asking to be reinstated. Someone was needed to supervise the construction of Bible school buildings as well as to teach in a large city in another country where the language the Browns knew was also spoken. Within a few months, the Browns had raised their support and were on their way. Although the boys again had to go to boarding school, it was only an hour away by road and they were able to spend many weekends together.

Less than a year later, the Browns had completely resigned from the mission and were back in the States, where Rich had taken a position at his alma mater. Rich's story was that he had been given a job to do but was not permitted to do it. He had gone out with the understanding that, besides being in charge of the construction, he would be director of the Bible school. However, another missionary was appointed director, bypassing Rich. The mission board said that Rich had overspent on the construction, that he had ordered thousands of dollars' worth of construction materials that had not been paid for, and that he had not given an accounting for much of the funds used. Rich's side of the story was spread throughout his district, causing friction until the whole story was told.

With Judy's nursing pay and Rich's salary, the family was soon able to afford a lovely home with a swimming pool. All three boys were doing well in school, although there were some discipline problems with the oldest. On the surface, they were an ideal couple with lovely children, active in church work. Then, with no warning, Rich ran off with his secretary. The shock to his family and parents was devastating. Since he could no longer work at the Bible college, he found work as a policeman. Judy, having to give up the home, moved into an apartment near her parents-in-law, who were very supportive of her and the boys. The oldest boy went to live with his father, had serious discipline problems, and completely stopped going to church, as had his father.

THE SMITHS

Ted Smith, raised in a happy Christian home on a modest farm in the northwestern part of the United States, felt a definite call from God to the Cape Verde Islands after a missionary from there ministered in his home church. From the time he was eleven, several preachers and evangelists prophesied to him that he would be used of the Lord in a special way, convincing him that he was being called into full-time ministry. After graduating from high school, he joined the army, following a family tradition, to save the funds necessary for Bible school.

During his time in basic training, he became actively involved in a Pentecostal church near the base, taking many of his army friends with him to services. Soon he was conducting a Bible study class to help new Christians grow in their spiritual experience. When he was transferred to another base, he became youth director in another Pentecostal church as well as a counselor in a drug rehabilitation program for young people. When orders came transferring him to Germany, he decided to marry his childhood sweetheart, Kathy, before leaving.

Within days of arriving in Germany, Ted was preaching in the Pentecostal church close to the base. Kathy joined Ted in Germany after graduating from high school a few months after their marriage. Shortly, both Ted and Kathy were working in an outstation of the original church, which started to grow in numbers, as well as conducting jail services. They decided that the Lord wanted them to continue ministry in Germany after Ted's discharge. However, Kathy became very ill and died of pneumonia just eight months after they had been married.

After his discharge, Ted became the youth pastor of a small Pentecostal church while supporting himself by working in the logging industry. Later that year, he enrolled in a Bible school. During his freshman year, Ted met and fell in love with Louise and they were married at the end of their sophomore year. When financial problems caused the Smiths to leave school, Ted was asked to become the pastor of a small church in the far Northwest, which he accepted. After two years, the church had almost tripled in size and the Smiths decided to finish their degrees in preparation for mission work.

Louise, also from a large Christian farm family, had accepted the Lord as Savior when she was six years old. Although she hadn't felt a definite call into full-time ministry, she had decided to go to Bible school for a year before entering secretarial school. There she had met and fell in love with Ted. From the very beginning of their friendship, Ted told her of his call to the mission field, specifically the Cape Verde Islands. As she prayed about their relationship, she came to the conclusion that if it was the Lord's will for her to marry Ted, then it was His will for her to go to the mission field as well.

Accepted as candidates by a Pentecostal denomination, the Smiths had little problem raising the needed support. Language study went well for both Ted and Louise, who arrived, happy and excited, on the field nine months later and twenty-one years after Ted had first felt the call to this country. Tears streamed down Ted's face as he walked down the ramp from the airplane.

The next hurdle was learning the local dialect, for all services and national church business were conducted in this language. By now Louise was involved in home schooling their two children, so she didn't have the time to spend in language study that Ted did. Although she had learned the official language well in language school, she never became fluent in the local dialect. Ted, in the meantime, thrived in his missionary activities. Since the national church was well organized with capable leadership, Ted did not have to become involved in administration but was able to spend all his time in evangelism, church planting, and discipling ministries.

The Smiths returned home for furlough after four years on the field. Deputation went well, the needed funds were raised, and the family returned to the Islands after a year. At the beginning of the second term, it seemed that Murphy's Law went into effect. First, their mission vehicle developed mechanical problems and seemed to be in the garage for repairs almost every month. The Smiths had always lived very simply, generally buying used furniture and appliances from missionaries going on furlough. They discovered that termites had destroyed a small used freezer and the old gas/electric refrigerator quit working. Their two boys became bored with home schooling and tired of having no social activities with peers from their own culture. The family tried to get them into the nearest mission boarding school, but there was no room.

About nine months after returning to the field, Ted developed muscle spasms in his back that became very painful. He had a number of tests done locally but no cause could be found. Louise was finding it more and more difficult to cope with the presence of national Christians in her home. Because they lived at the mission station, there seemed to be almost constant activity, which left her with little privacy. She also found the dry, dusty heat difficult to bear. Sometimes she felt a little abandoned because she had to cope with home problems while Ted was ministering in seminars in other parts of the country.

During this time there were uprisings in several African countries and a number of missionaries had to leave for fear of being killed. Although the political situation was calm in the Islands, Louise began wondering what would happen to her and the boys if they were suddenly evacuated while Ted was away from home.

Ted returned to the States for further tests but the doctors could find no cause for the pain he was suffering. Two months later his wife and children joined him. The Smiths' mission board has a very lenient medical leave policy and was eager to work with Ted and Louise to help them through this difficult time. The regional director had telephoned the family many times while on the field. But only a few weeks after his wife arrived in the States, Ted called the office to resign, giving no reason other than medical. When talking with friends, Ted indicated that he had resigned because of concern for his family. Although he still feels called to the mission field, he does not believe that he will ever be able to return. He is hoping to find a church to pastor somewhere in the northwestern part of the United States. Louise felt that perhaps the Lord was using adverse circumstances to lead them into a different ministry.

Both Ted and Louise indicated that they loved the national church leaders and missionaries they were working with. They feel no animosity toward the mission board. At the same time, they did not go to the home office for a debriefing and no one from the home office visited them after their return to America.

THE HAMILTONS

Don Hamilton was his parents' pride and joy. Having accepted Christ as his Savior at a young age, he was constantly involved in children's and young people's ministries in his father's church. Handsome, personable, with an outstanding baritone voice, Don was popular with all the Christian youth in the area. Don's father died suddenly of a heart attack during Don's sophomore year in high school, but Don continued to minister in the church under the new pastor.

Linda's parents attended the same church, so the two young people grew up knowing each other and fell in love while they were still in high school. Linda, too, had a lovely voice and she and Don were often asked to sing at special youth functions. However, problems between Linda's parents resulted in divorce. Linda's mother continued to be faithful to the church, supporting herself and her daughter from her salary as a beautician.

Don and Linda were married during their senior year in high school, finding consolation in each other after the tragedies in their families. Don had felt a call to the mission field so he applied and was accepted at a Bible college near their home. Linda worked to help with finances until the birth of their first child. Because of their singing, the young couple were often asked to minister in churches throughout the area. They were also active in youth ministry and Don accepted a position as youth pastor when he graduated. A second daughter was born during this time.

Don greatly admired a missionary from their church who, because he was a pilot, was able to pioneer churches in remote areas of South America. Don took flying lessons and soon had his private pilot's license. The missionary's wife, who was a nurse, encouraged Linda to go to nursing school, not only to be better prepared to take care of her own girls on the mission field but also to be able to help the local people. Although Linda had no education beyond high school, she did very well in nursing, managing to complete the requirements to become a registered nurse while still caring for her family.

The couple decided that they should accept the pastorate of a small church to fulfill the prerequisites of their denomination for missionary service. The church grew under Don's gregarious, outgoing ministry, but it was also apparent that Don, not the church board, was firmly in control. It seemed that the firm control extended to his family as well. He continued in a close, supportive relationship with his mother, who did not remarry.

As soon as the required two years of ministry were completed, the couple applied for missionary appointment and were accepted. Well-known in the district, the Hamiltons had little trouble raising the necessary support. They were able to sell thousands of their singing tapes in the churches they visited to help obtain the funds and within a year were on their way to language school. Both Don and Linda did well learning Spanish, as did their children, who attended a local preschool.

During this time, Don's denomination decided not to invest any more funds in planes, selling the few remaining in service. But there was a desperate need in the country the Hamiltons were going to for someone to run the radio studio, which made tapes in a number of local Indian dialects. These tapes were aired throughout the country on local radio stations and seemed to be having an impact in areas where there were no churches. Since Don and Linda were familiar with recording, they accepted the challenge of this ministry.

The first six months in their host country were spent in finding and renovating a house for the family. Although the city where the Hamiltons were ministering was less than an hour's drive from a missionary boarding and day school in the capital city, Don decided that Linda should home school their two daughters. They prepared one room in the house as a schoolroom, bringing from America all the books and supplies needed for three years. Although Linda tried to keep a regimented teaching schedule, it became more and more difficult with the constant company Don invited to their home.

Don was also very particular about their food. Although fresh fruit and vegetables were readily available in the large local markets in the capital city, as well as in a number of grocery stores that carried basic food items, the Hamiltons had brought several drums of dried and canned foodstuff from America. They had also brought a number of household appliances with them and consequently decided that Linda would do all the housework instead of hiring a local domestic.

Don enjoyed ministering in the large Spanish-speaking church in the capital whenever he was invited. The educated, middle-class congregation seemed to enjoy the Hamiltons' ministry as well. Because no national pastor could be found for the church when it was time for the missionary pastor to go on furlough, the Hamiltons were asked to transfer to the city to take this ministry. Both Don and Linda seemed happy to make the transfer, enjoying all the benefits of big-city living. It was no longer necessary to home school the girls; they could now attend the American mission academy, leaving Linda free to minister in the church to the women and children.

The Hamiltons left for furlough a year later, apparently happy with their ministry and looking forward to returning. However, toward the end of their furlough, Don asked for and was granted permission to transfer to Spain to work in the newly developed media-ministry office for all Spanish-speaking countries. The couple left in August in plenty of time to get settled in a new home before the girls started school in the local English-speaking international school. Don fitted into the high-pressure media office situation with enthusiasm, enjoying ministry in local churches as well as the challenge of creating programs for radio and television.

About four months later, Don returned home to find a note from Linda. She had returned to the States with their two daughters. The note said he had had his life and now she wanted to have hers. No other explanation was given. By the time Don arrived in America, Linda had already filed for divorce. Linda would not talk with any of the personnel from the mission board, nor would she consider counseling. Don insisted that he had no idea why Linda had left him. Linda worked as a nurse to support herself and her daughters. Don moved in with his mother while ministering again in the church where he had been the youth pastor. He became very involved in the singles ministry where he met and married a divorcée. That marriage lasted for a very short time; there seemed to be unresolvable differences of opinion. After that, Don quit going to church; he couldn't face the humiliation of having failed a second time.

When the Hamiltons' missionary compatriots were asked if they had sensed any problems, only a few facts came to light.

Don had often commented that some people had to sacrifice more than others to come to the mission field. He felt that he could have made a good living in the States as a pilot but he had given that up because of God's call. Few had heard Linda complain, but she had asked a friend for any books available on pride.

Case Studies

Bibliography

ARTICLES

Allen, Frank. "Making Room for the New Generation." *Evangelical Missions Quarterly* 25 (October 1989): 395–98.

_____, "Why Do They Leave? Reflections on Attrition." *Evangelical Missions Quarterly* 22 (April 1986): 118–28.

Bacon, Daniel W. "The Tin-Cup Image Can Be Shattered." *Evangelical Missions Quarterly* 22 (October 1986): 376–78.

Bonk, Jon. "Affluence: The Achilles' Heel of Missions." *Evangelical Missions Quarterly* 21 (October 1985): 383–90.

Britt, William Gordon III. "Pretraining Variables in the Prediction of Missionary Success Overseas." *Journal of Psychology and Theology* 11 (Fall 1983): 203–12.

Camburn, Dave. "The Conservative Baptist Foreign Mission Society." *Evangelical Missions Quarterly* 22 (April 1986): 127–28.

Chester, Raymond M. "Stress on Missionary Families Living in 'Other Culture' Situations." *Journal of Psychology and Christianity* 2, no. 4 (Winter 1983): 30–37.

Chiang, Samuel E. "Partnerships at the Crossroads: Red, Yellow, or Green Light?" *Evangelical Missions Quarterly* 28 (July 1992): 284–89.

Congdon, G. Dal. "Retiring Missionaries, Gold Mine of Workers for North American Cross-Cultural Ministry." *Evangelical Missions Quarterly* 25 (April 1989): 176–81.

Cook, Clyde. "Why the Opportunity for Unproductiveness?" *Evangelical Missions Quarterly* 26 (July 1990): 251–53.

Articles **167**

Coote, Robert T. "A Boon or a 'Drag'? How North American Evangelical Missionaries Experience Home Furloughs." *International Bulletin of Missionary Research* 15 (January 1991): 17–23.

Cummings, David. "Programmed for Failure—Mission Candidates at Risk." *Evangelical Missions Quarterly* 23 (July 1987): 240–46.

Diekhoff, George M., Bruce A. Holder, Phil Colee, Phil Wigginton, and Faye Rees. "The Ideal Overseas Missionary: A Cross-Cultural Comparison." *Journal of Psychology and Theology* 19 (Summer 1991): 178–85.

Dixon, Janice. "Unrealistic Expectations: The Downfall of Many Missionaries." *Evangelical Missions Quarterly* 26 (October 1990): 388–93.

Donovan, Kath. "'Beauty for Ashes'—Redeeming Premature Field Departure." *Evangelical Missions Quarterly* 27 (January 1991): 18–22.

Downes, R. F. "A Look at the Third Culture Child." *The Japan Christian Quarterly* (Spring 1976): 68–71.

Dubert, Karen. "Ten Steps to Success: The Major Themes." *Evangelical Missions Quarterly* 25 (April 1989): 161–63.

Foyle, Marjory. "Burnout or Brownout?" *Evangelical Missions Quarterly* 22 (July 1986): 262–70.

————. "Gorillas Get Along: Why Can't We?" *Evangelical Missions Quarterly* 22 (January 1986): 14–20.

————. "Missionary Relationships: Powderkeg or Powerhouse?" *Evangelical Missions Quarterly* 21 (October 1985): 342–49.

————. "Why It's Tough to Get Along with Each Other." *Evangelical Missions Quarterly* 21 (July 1985): 240–45.

Frisbey, Norman. "Retirement of Evangelical Missionaries: Elements of Satisfaction and Morale." *Journal of Psychology and Theology* 15 (Winter 1987): 326–35.

Gangel, Kenneth O. "Developing New Leaders for the Global Task." *Evangelical Missions Quarterly* 25 (April 1989): 166–71.

Gardner, Laura Mae. "Proactive Care of Missionary Personnel." *Journal of Psychology and Theology* 15 (Winter 1987): 308–14.

Gish, Dorothy J. "Sources of Missionary Stress." *Journal of Psychology and Theology* 11 (Fall 1983): 236–42.

Gundykunst, William B., Mitchell R. Hammer, and Richard L. Wiseman. "An Analysis of an Integrated Approach to Cross-Cultural Training." *International Journal of Intercultural Relations* 1 (Spring 1977): 107–8.

Herndon, Helen Louise. "How Many 'Dropouts' Really Are 'Pushouts'?" *Evangelical Missions Quarterly* 16 (January 1980): 13–15.

Bibliography

Bibliography

Hill, Harriet. "Incarnational Ministry: A Critical Examination." *Evangelical Missions Quarterly* 26 (April 1990): 196–201.

Hunter, William F., and Marvin K. Mayers. "Psychology and Missions: Reflections on Status and Need." *Journal of Psychology and Theology* 15 (Winter 1987): 269–73.

Jones, Marge. "First-Year Counseling: A Key Ingredient to Success." *Evangelical Missions Quarterly* 29 (July 1993): 294–97.

Jourard, Sydney. "Some Psychological Aspects of Privacy." *Law and Contemporary Problems* (Spring 1966).

Lewis, K. "Creative Concerns for Important Kids." *In Other Words* 9, no. 8 (1983): 1.

Loewen, Jacob A. "Roles Relating to an Alien Social Structure." *Missiology: An International Review* 4 (April 1976): 217–42.

Mace, David R., and Vera C. Mace. "Marriage Enrichment for Clergy Couples." *Pastoral Psychology* 30 (Spring 1982): 151–59.

Mackin, Sandra L. "Multinational Teams: Smooth as Silk or Rough as Rawhide?" *Evangelical Missions Quarterly* 28 (April 1992): 134–40.

McElhanon, Kenneth. "Don't Give Up on the Incarnational Model." *Evangelical Missions Quarterly* 27 (October 1991): 390–93.

Nelson, D. Kurt. "There Are Some Workable Alternatives to the Old Way of Doing Deputation." *Evangelical Missions Quarterly* 15 (October 1986): 365–71.

Nelson, Paul. "Home Schooling in the Missions Context." *Evangelical Missions Quarterly* 24 (April 1988): 126–29.

Nussbaum, Stan. "Relationships May Precede Economic Adjustments." *Evangelical Missions Quarterly* 21 (October 1985): 392–93.

Oberg, Kalervo. "Cultural Shock: Adjustment to New Cultural Environments." *Practical Anthropology* 7 (1960): 177–82.

Parshall, Phil. "Why Some People Are Unproductive." *Evangelical Missions Quarterly* 26 (July 1990): 246–51.

Plueddmann, James E. "The Issue Is Love, Not Affluence." *Evangelical Missions Quarterly* 21 (October 1985): 392–93.

Pocock, Michael. "The Evangelical Alliance Mission." *Evangelical Missions Quarterly* 22 (April 1986): 122–25.

"Politicians and Privacy." *CQ Researcher* 17 (April 1992): 338.

Pollock, David C. "Strategies for Dealing with Crisis in Missionary Kid Education." *International Bulletin of Missionary Research* 13, no. 1 (January 1989): 14–19.

Renich, Fred C. "First-Term Objectives." *Evangelical Missions Quarterly* 3 (Summer 1967): 209–17.

Rogers, Carl R. "The Concept of the Fully Functioning Person." *Psychotherapy* 1 (1963): 17–26.

Sall, Millard J. "Demon Possession or Psychopathology? A Clinical Differentiation." *Journal of Psychology and Theology* 4 (Fall 1976): 286–90.

Sharp, Larry. "Boarding Schools: What Difference Do They Make?" *Evangelical Missions Quarterly* 26 (January 1990): 26–35.

Sharp, Larry W. "Toward a Greater Understanding of the Real MK: A Review of Recent Research." *Journal of Psychology and Christianity* 4 (1985): 73–78.

Smith, Stan, "The Trouble with My Home Board Is . . . " *Evangelical Missions Quarterly* 21 (April 1985): 119–31.

Vaage, Leif E. "On Being a Missionary: Models of Self-understanding." *Missiology: An International Review* 17 (April 1989): 131–41.

Ward, Ted. "The Anxious Climate of Concern for Missionary Children." *International Bulletin of Missionary Research* 13, no. 1 (January 1989): 11–13.

White, Frances J. "Some Reflections on the Separation Phenomenon Idiosyncratic to the Experience of Missionaries and Their Children." *Journal of Psychology and Theology* 11 (Fall 1983): 181–88.

White, Frances J., and Elaine M. Nesbit. "Separation: Balancing the Gains and Losses." *Evangelical Missions Quarterly* 22 (October 1986): 393–97.

Wickstrom, David Lee, and J. Roland Fleck. "Missionary Children: Correlates of Self-esteem and Dependency." *Journal of Psychology and Theology* 11 (Fall 1983): 226–35.

BOOKS

Becker, Arthur H. *Guilt: Curse or Blessing?* Minneapolis: Augsburg Publishing House, 1977.

Bernard, Harold W., and Wesley C. Huckins. *Dynamics of Personal Adjustment.* Boston: Holbrook Press, 1975.

Bowlby, J. *Attachment and Loss.* Vol. 3. New York: Basic Books, 1980.

Bradshaw, John. *Healing the Shame That Binds You.* Dearfield Beach, Fla.: Health Communications, 1988.

Brewster, E. Thomas, and Elizabeth S. Brewster. *Bonding and the Missionary Task.* Pasadena, Calif.: Lingua House, 1982.

Buffam, C. John. *The Life and Times of an MK.* Pasadena, Calif.: William Carey Library, 1985.

Bibliography

Collins, G. *You Can Profit from Stress.* Santa Ana, Calif.: Vision House, 1977.

Craig, Grace J. *Human Development.* 5th ed. Englewood Cliffs, N.J.: Prentice Hall, 1989.

Dayton, Edward R., ed. *Mission Handbook: North American Protestant Ministries Overseas.* 10th ed. Monrovia, Calif.: Missions Advanced Research & Communications Center, 1973.

DiCaprio, Nicholas S. *Personality Theories: A Guide to Human Nature.* 2d ed. New York: Holt, Rinehart and Winston, 1983.

Dodd, Carley H. *Dynamics of Intercultural Communication.* 2d ed. Dubuque: William C. Brown, 1987.

Drakeford, John W. *Integrity Therapy.* Nashville: Broadman Press, 1967.

Echerd, Pam, and Alice Arathoon, eds. *Planning for MK Nurture.* Vol. 2. Pasadena, Calif.: William Carey Library, 1989.

Foyle, Marjory F. *Overcoming Missionary Stress.* Wheaton, Ill.: Evangelical Missions Information Service, 1987.

Furnham, Adrian, and Stephen Bochner. *Culture Shock: Psychological Reactions to Unfamiliar Environments.* London: Methuen, 1986.

Goode, Stephen. *The Right to Privacy.* New York: Franklin Watts, 1983.

Harcum, E. Rae. *Psychology for Daily Living: Simple Guidance in Human Relations for Parents, Teachers, and Others.* Chicago: Nelson-Hall, 1979.

Hodges, Melvin L. *The Indigenous Church.* Springfield, Mo.: Gospel Publishing House, 1953.

Houselander, Caryll. *Guilt.* New York: Sheed & Ward, 1951.

Howard, J. Grant. *The Trauma of Transparency.* Portland, Oreg.: Multnomah Press, 1979.

Keidel, Levi. *Stop Treating Me Like God.* Carol Stream, Ill.: Creation House, 1971.

Knight, James A. *Conscience and Guilt.* New York: Appelton-Century-Crofts, 1969.

Knowles, Malcolm. *The Adult Learner: A Neglected Species.* 2d ed. Houston, Tex.: Gulf Publishing, 1979.

Larson, Donald N. *Guidelines for Barefoot Language Learning.* St. Paul, Minn.: CMS Publishing, 1984.

Larson, Donald N., and William A. Smalley. *Becoming Bilingual: A Guide to Language Learning.* Pasadena, Calif.: William Carey Library, 1972.

Loss, Myron. *Culture Shock: Dealing with Stress in Cross-Cultural Living.* Winona Lake, Ind.: Light and Life Press, 1983.

Mayers, Marvin Keene. *Christianity Confronts Culture; a Strategy for Cross-Cultural Evangelism.* Grand Rapids: Zondervan Publishing House, 1974.

McGee, Robert S. *The Search for Significance.* 2d ed. Houston, Tex.: Rapha Publishing, 1990.

Miner, John B. *Personnel Psychology.* London: Collier-Macmillan, 1969.

Narramore, Bruce, and Bill Counts. *Guilt and Freedom.* Santa Ana, Calif.: Vision House Publishers, 1974.

Narramore, S. Bruce. *No Condemnation: Rethinking Guilt Motivation in Counseling, Preaching and Parenting.* Grand Rapids: Zondervan Publishing House, 1984.

Oden, Thomas C. *Guilt Free.* Nashville: Abingdon, 1980.

O'Donnell, Kelly S., and Michele Lewis O'Donnell, eds. *Helping Missionaries Grow: Readings in Mental Health and Missions.* Pasadena, Calif.: William Carey Library, 1988.

Papalia, Diane E., and Sally W. Olds. *Psychology.* New York: McGraw-Hill, 1988.

Rathus, Spencer A. *Psychology.* 2d ed. New York: Holt, Rinehart and Winston, 1984.

Reed, Lyman E. *Preparing Missionaries for Intercultural Communication.* Pasadena, Calif.: William Carey Library, 1985.

Rubin, Joan, and Irene Thompson. *How to Be a More Successful Language Learner.* Boston: Heinle & Heinle Publishers, 1982.

Schroeder, Beverly A. *Human Growth and Development.* St. Paul, Minn.: West Publishing, 1992.

Schulz, Richard, and Robert B. Ewen. *Adult Development and Aging.* New York: Macmillan Publishing, 1993.

Silverman, Robert E. *Psychology.* Englewood Cliffs, N.J.: Prentice-Hall, 1978.

Slough, M. C. *Privacy, Freedom and Responsibility.* Springfield, Ill.: Charles C. Thomas, 1969.

Smith, Donald K. *Creating Understanding.* Grand Rapids: Zondervan Publishing House, 1991.

Stevenson-Moessner, Jeanne. *Theological Dimensions of Maturation in a Missionary Milieu.* New York: Peter Lang, 1989.

Tournier, Paul. *Guilt and Grace: A Psychological Study.* New York: Harper and Row, 1962.

Trevor-Roper, H. R. *The Last Days of Hitler.* New York: Macmillan, 1947.

Bibliography

Bibliography

Williams, Kenneth L. "Resolving Conflicts in Christian Marriage." In *Helping Missionaries Grow: Readings in Mental Health and Missions,* eds. Kelly S. O'Donnell and Michele Lewis O'Donnell, 211–18. Pasadena, Calif.: William Carey Library, 1988.

Williams, Morris O. *Partnership in Missions: A Study of Theology and Method in Mission.* Springfield, Mo.: Empire Printing, 1979.

DISSERTATIONS

Iwasko, Ronald A. "An Integrated Program for Training First-Term Missionaries of the Assemblies of God." D.Miss. diss., Trinity Evangelical Divinity School, 1984.

Rosedale, Roy S. "Cross-Cultural Missionary Training; Biblical Basis and Model." Ph.D. diss., California Graduate School of Theology, 1981.

Subject Index